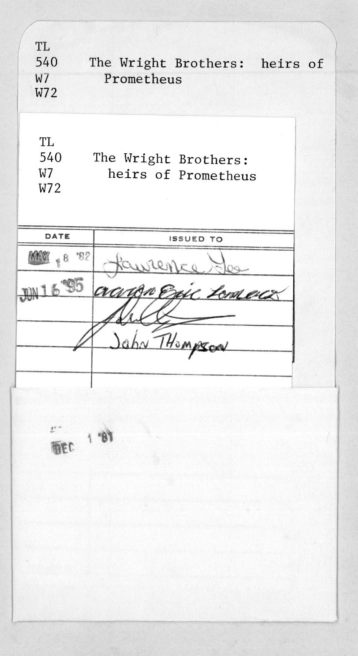

"By far the greatest obstacle to the progress of science and to the undertaking of new tasks and provinces therein, is found in this — that men despair and think things impossible."

FRANCIS BACON

"It is therefore incontestably the Wright brothers alone who resolved, in its entirety, the problem of human mechanical flight ... Men of genius — erudite, exact in their reasoning, hard workers, outstanding experimenters, and unselfish ... They changed the face of the globe."

CHARLES DOLLFUS

Wilbur and Orville Wright, 1912

The WRIGHT BROTHERS

Heirs of Prometheus

Edited by
RICHARD P. HALLION
Curator of Science and Technology
National Air and Space Museum

with contributions by
ROGER E. BILSTEIN
TOM D. CROUCH
PAUL E. GARBER
CHARLES H. GIBBS-SMITH
MARVIN W. McFARLAND
DOMINICK A. PISANO
MELVIN B. ZISFEIN

Published by the
National Air and Space Museum
Smithsonian Institution

Distributed by the
Smithsonian Institution Press
Washington City
1978

Library of Congress Cataloging in Publication Data

The Wright Brothers: Heirs of Prometheus

   Lectures presented at a symposium
commemorating the 75th anniversary of the
Wright brothers' first powered, sustained and
controlled, heavier-than-air flight in 1903. The
symposium was held December 14, 1978, and
was sponsored by the National Air and Space
Museum.
   Bibliography: p.
   1. Wright, Orville, 1871-1948. 2. Wright,
Wilbur, 1867-1912. I. Bilstein, Roger E. II.
Hallion, Richard. TL540.W7W72
629.13'0092'2 [B] 78-606141

ISBN 0-87474-504-7

ISBN 0-87474-503-9 pbk.

Cover illustrations:

Front jacket: The 1908 Wright Flyer being
flown by Orville Wright at Ft. Myer, Virginia.

Back jacket: The 1911 Wright glider at Kitty
Hawk, North Carolina, flown by Orville Wright.

Designed by Gerard A. Valerio,
Bookmark Studio

Composed in Bookman by
General Typographers, Inc.

Printed on Hamilton offset by the John D.
Lucas Printing Co.

Table of Contents

Acknowledgments

The publication of any edited volume is dependent upon the cooperative efforts of many individuals. The following were of great assistance during the preparation of this work. Michael Collins and Melvin B. Zisfein, Director and Deputy Director of the National Air and Space Museum, conceived of this symposium, and encouraged the editor at every stage. The Assistant Directors of the museum, Frederick Durant III, Donald Lopez, and Dr. Howard Wolko, provided constant and unfailing cooperation. Executive Officer John Whitelaw and M. Antoinette Smith were instrumental in arranging for the publication of the work. Dr. Tom D. Crouch, Curator of Astronautics, and Charles H. Gibbs-Smith, Lindbergh Professor of Aerospace History at the NASM, assisted in photograph selection and offered many helpful suggestions. Catherine Scott, NASM Librarian, greatly facilitated photographic and bibliographic research. Felix C. Lowe, Deputy Director of the Smithsonian Institution Press, arranged for editing, design, and publication services. The manuscript was edited by Peter Rohrbach, and the volume was designed by Gerard Valerio. Special thanks are due Lillian Kozloski, Barbara Pawlowski, and Diane Pearson, who typed the manuscript.

Foreword

MELVIN B. ZISFEIN

Anyone can change the world irreversibly. To greater or lesser extent, creatures of this earth are continuously and irreversibly changing both their environment and each other. However, at vastly infrequent intervals—by the way we humans perceive time—comes a change so fundamental, so innovative, so pervasive, that most old ways can be no more. Methods of doing business, of helping each other, of enjoying our leisure, are changed for all time.

Such was the invention of powered heavier-than-air flight. What can we say here that has not been said repeatedly since 1903? How, on this seventy-fifth anniversary of flight, can we add to the general perception of the grandeur and the brilliance of the Wrights' insight? How, even though we want to startle the world with the fantastic genius of these two learned, methodical, taciturn, and sober brothers, can we produce some astounding revelation that will bring the public to its feet? Obviously we cannot. We can only restate, amplify, supplement, and burnish with the perspective of 75 years the story that we know so well. We do so in the hope that our telling will take us closer to the full appreciation due the two geniuses from Dayton and this phenomenon called powered heavier-than-air flight. By their triumph, they changed both our world and us dramatically—and for all time.

MELVIN B. ZISFEIN is Acting Director of the National Air and Space Museum. A native of Philadelphia, Pennsylvania, Mr. Zisfein pursued an Honors Program at the Massachusetts Institute of Technology, simultaneously receiving his bachelor of science and master of science degrees in aeronautical engineering in 1948. Mr. Zisfein worked for various aerospace companies as an aircraft designer and aerodynamicist. He joined the Bell Aircraft Corporation in 1953, becoming chief of the dynamics department. In 1960, he became the general manager of the astromechanics research division of Giannini Controls Corporation. In 1966 he was named Associate Director of the Franklin Institute Research Laboratories. In March 1971, Mr. Zisfein joined the Smithsonian Institution as Deputy Director of the National Air and Space Museum. In 1977 he was awarded the Smithsonian's Exceptional Service Gold Medal for the development of the museum's exhibits. He was named Acting Director of the National Air and Space Museum on April 24, 1978.

Introduction

Two of the giants in the American Pantheon of popular heroes are the brothers Wilbur and Orville Wright. On December 17, 1903, they fulfilled the dream of centuries by successfully completing the world's first powered, sustained, and controlled flight in aviation history.

A remarkable record of that event exists: a photograph, taken just after the Wright Flyer has lifted from its launching rail. The Flyer is in full, steady flight, with Orville, the pilot, using the deflected canard elevator to climb away from the ground. His brother Wilbur, visibly tense with excitement, is posed in a dynamic stance, watching the Flyer soar along. What makes the photograph so remarkable is its record of a dramatic, world-shaping change in technology; this frail-looking kite-like biplane will eventually lead to intercontinental jet airliners, as well as new and frightening military weapons. That flight one cold and blustery December day changed the world permanently.

Above all, the flight was not the product of chance, or luck, or two tinkerers. The Wrights did not suddenly and simply decide to go from making bicycles to making airplanes. Rather, they were brilliant, intuitive flight researchers. They recognized the vital importance of blending theory and ground research with research aloft. They realized that the critical problems of flight were those that concerned control and piloting, and not just the obvious ones of lift and propulsion. They recognized that at some point one had to leave the drawing board for the sky. Wilbur Wright, for example, compared the development of an airplane to riding a fractious horse. "If you are looking for perfect safety," he stated, "you will do well to sit on a fence and watch the birds, but if you really wish to learn you must mount a machine and become acquainted with its tricks by actual trial."

While others invested sums in untried contraptions and various hasty schemes, the Wrights patiently set to work. They read voluminously. They studied birds. They corresponded with leading aeronautical figures, such as Octave Chanute. They built a wind tunnel and experimented with various wing shapes. They build manned kites, and then gliders. With the 1902-1903

Wright glider, they perfected methods of flight control so that they could exercise effective three-axis control in roll, pitch, and yaw. Now, at last, they were ready to blend their aerodynamic and structural configuration with a suitable powerplant. The result was the epochal 1903 Flyer, the world's first successful airplane. Seen today in the Milestones of Flight exhibit gallery of the National Air and Space Museum, it appears unbelievably crude. It represented, however, the highest standards of technological creativity, and the Flyer is the ancestor of all modern winged flight vehicles.

Though they lacked formal engineering training, the Wright brothers can be viewed as later examples of the nineteenth century's "heroic engineer" figure—the Roebling or Brunel who shatters past traditions and establishes a new mold in technology. Indeed, the Wrights had gone far beyond any comparable figure. They remained ahead of the rest of the world — notably Europe — and it was only after others saw the Wright aircraft at close hand and understood the reasoning behind them that they were able to proceed successfully along their own development paths.

In part, because of the well-publicized failures of such individuals as Samuel Langley, the public was not willing to accept the possibility of powered heavier-than-air flight. Amos Root's quaint account in *Gleanings in Bee Culture* of seeing Wilbur Wright fly in 1904 was little noted, and the Wrights, concerned about perfecting their aircraft, were content with the lack of publicity that surrounded their efforts. In 1908, a climatic year, Orville demonstrated the Wright aircraft to the U.S. Army at Ft. Myer, Virginia. His brother Wilbur stunned European aviators the same year by demonstrating sustained and controlled flights during a European tour. European aviation, which had been in decline since the death of Lilienthal and Pilcher, was reborn, on the basis of Wright technology.

In the United States, the Wrights were joined by a new host of aircraft developers, individuals such as Curtiss, Martin, and Boeing, names that would add their own luster to the annals of world aviation. Tragically, Wilbur Wright died in 1912 of typhoid fever. His brother Orville lived on, the doyen of American aviation pioneers, until his death in 1948. That same year, in accordance with Orville Wright's wishes, the historic 1903 Wright Flyer, which had been on exhibit at the Science Museum, London, was returned to the United States and placed on exhibit in the Smithsonian Institution.

The papers included in this volume present the reflections of a group of uniquely qualified scholars on the achievements of the Wrights 75 years after Kitty Hawk. They stand both as a tribute to the two brothers from Dayton, and as a contribution towards a greater appreciation of the revolution that occurred above Kill Devil Hill, a revolution whose reverberations are still being felt today.

Often it is the outsider who alone possesses the necessary detachment from a subject to enunciate most clearly the significance or a particular development or event. And so it is with the Wrights. Writing in 1923, Le Corbusier, the great exponent of the "modern movement" in architecture, stated: "We may then affirm that the airplane mobilized invention, intelligence, and daring: *imagination* and *cold reason.* It is the same spirit that built the Parthenon."[1]

1. Le Corbusier. *Towards a New Architecture.* trans. by Frederick Etchells (New York, 1970), p. 101.

RICHARD P. HALLION, Curator of Science and Technology at the National Air and Space Museum, is a native of Washington, D.C. He received his Ph.D. in history from the University of Maryland in 1975. Dr. Hallion is the author of *Supersonic Flight: Breaking the Sound Barrier and Beyond* (1972), and *Legacy of Flight: The Guggenheim Contribution to American Aviation* (1977), as well as numerous articles and monographs. He won the 1975 History Manuscript Award of the American Institute of Aeronautics and Astronautics. He holds joint appointments with the University College and the Department of Aerospace Engineering, University of Maryland.

The WRIGHT BROTHERS

Heirs of Prometheus

Aeronautics in the Pre-Wright Era

Engineers and the Airplane

TOM D. CROUCH

There is not a shred of doubt that Wilbur and Orville Wright invented the airplane in a much truer sense than Morse invented the telegraph or Edison the incandescent light bulb. By virtue of their brilliant technical insight and engineering genius they overcame the problems that had long blocked the route to a successful airplane. They cut straight to the heart of the matter that their predecessors had either skirted or attacked from a totally incorrect point of view. They undertook crucial quantitative analyses in essential areas where other experimenters had assumed the accuracy of available data. In essence, they functioned more successfully as engineers than men with the best formal training and many years of experience.

The very magnitude of the Wright achievement has tended to cloud our view of early aeronautical endeavor. Popular accounts present the two brothers as isolated geniuses who attacked a problem considered virtually insoluble by most established authorities in the scientific and technical professions. According to legend, they worked alone: untutored (if enormously talented) amateurs who enjoyed little or no contact with the better trained men who remained blind to the possibilities of a new technology. For many writers, the Wrights epitomize a heroic tradition of American invention, in which humble rural lads rose to greatness by solving mechanical problems that had been ignored by formally educated scientists and engineers for generations.[1]

This oversimplified view masks the central role played by professional technicians in the invention of the airplane during the four decades prior to 1903. The impact of the engineer on aviation had, in fact, been so profound that those in search of the origin of the airplane can virtually ignore events that occured prior to the advent of the technical professional to the field. Far from having abandoned flight studies to amateur mechanics, these men

1. In view of the very real need to establish the basic question of Wright priority and to demonstrate the brillance of their achievement, this overemphasis on the brothers as solitary pioneers is not too difficult to understand. Nevertheless, the resulting point of view has masked the real importance of the engineering profession in early aeronautics.

3

displaced the cranks and eccentrics who had dominated aeronautics for centuries.

The flying machine enthusiast of 1800 stood as far from his goal as had that remote ancestor who first envied the freedom of the birds. This realization helps to explain one of the most remarkable puzzles in the history of flight. Why did it take so long to devise a machine capable of carrying a human being away from the surface of the earth? Flight, after all, is one of mankind's oldest aspirations. The dream of flight, the desire to emulate the "way of the eagle in the air," is so deeply rooted in antiquity that it seems almost to have been innate.

Aeronautical historians have long assumed that this deep-seated desire to fly led countless individuals throughout the centuries to don makeshift wings and make semi-suicidal leaps from high places. In fact, the number of men alleged to have attempted flight in this manner is remarkably small, given the extent to which the dream prevaded religion, literature, and folk culture. The absence of any evidence suggesting the existence of even the simplest flying toys in antiquity, moreover, is remarkable in a cultural group that apparently yearned to fly.

The depth of this paradox — a desire to fly coupled with so little progress toward the goal over several millenia — becomes even more evident when it is realized that mankind could have ventured aloft in simple hang gliders or free balloons constructed solely of materials readily available in antiquity. Nor would our ancient aviators have required a sophisticated understanding of the physical principles underlying flight. All of the necessary basics could have been derived empirically through a process of trial and error.

It is, in fact, entirely possible that a few isolated individuals did come close to limited success with flying machines in the distant past, only to be ignored or ridiculed by their contemporaries. Lynn White argues persuasively for a long glide by Eilmer, an 11th century Benedictine monk of Malmesbury Abbey.[2] Six hundred years later John Wilkins, Bishop of Chester, founding member of the Royal Society and brother-in-law of Oliver Cromwell, provided an even more striking account of a fellow who seems to have been well on his way with a flight test program that presaged the methods of Otto Lilienthal three centuries later. Bishop Wilkins remarked that somewhere in England there was a man capable of making glides of up to 300 feet, a distance considered most creditable by the gliding pioneers of the late 19th century. Yet the author, a man with enormous interest in all phases of science and technology, not only refused to investigate this wonder, but did not even bother to discover the name of this unheralded pioneer. The significance of the achievement was obviously lost on him. A similar situation exists in the

2. Lynn White, "Eilmer of Malmesbury: An Eleventh Century Aviatior," *Technology and Culture,* p. 3 (Spring 1972), 98.

3. John Wilkins, *Mathematical Magic: or the Wonders That May Be Performed by Mechanical Geometry* (London, 1948) in *The Natural and Philosophical Works of the Right Reverend John Wilkins* (London, 1970), p. 193.

case of lighter-than-air flight.[3] As early as 1420, at least one European had provided a reasonably accurate description of a man-carrying hot air or smoke balloon, but his only reward was the ridicule of his peers.[4]

The unknown glider and balloon builders of these accounts faced enormous technical problems. Nevertheless, their work might have served as a starting point for a flight research program culminating in the eventual development of hang gliders that could have permitted the further exploration of aerodynamic and structural problems.

Such was not to be the case, however, for social, cultural, and intellectual factors prevented the establishment of such programs. The refusal of the most astute thinkers in science and technology to express a serious interest in the possibility of flight was a particularly telling blow, ensuring that talented technicians would receive little encouragement to enter the field. The absence of leadership was also a key element preventing the growth of lines of communications that would build a sense of cooperation and lead to a coordinated, systematic approach to the subject. Finally, no real progress could be made until technicians evolved a framework that would enable them to recognize relationships between isolated bits of information, to study the development of problem areas, and to chart the most promising avenues toward success. In essence, aeronautics required an organized, coordinated, ongoing effort to assess and draw maximum benefit from the contributions of individual experimenters.

Sir George Cayley, "the Father of Aerial Navigation" began the process that culminated in the provision of these missing elements. Born at Scarborough in 1773, Cayley's career marks the first real watershed in the history of flight. He was the first to apply the methodology of science to flight technology. His work fixed the basic configuration of the modern airplane and suggested the all-important separation of the lift, propulsion and control systems. Nor were his efforts restricted to theory and publication. On the basis of his findings, he constructed the world's first successful model glider and two full scale machines capable of flight with a pilot aboard.

Not all of Cayley's work shows such prescience, however. Designs that bear the mark of genius are mixed in his notebooks with ornithopters and man-powered aircraft that represent a decided retrogression. He also seems to have been totally unwilling to abandon outmoded paddles and flappers for the propeller. The failure of a man of Cayley's undoubted genius to mount a long term flight research program culminating in the development of an efficient glider is perhaps the most persuasive evidence of the need for a concerted attack on the problems of flight by a larger number of men with broad technical experience. Nevertheless, after millenia of neglect, Cayley had taken the first step toward the realization of the dream. The interest, enthusiasm

4. Clive Hart, *The Dream of Flight: Aeronautics From Classical Times to the Rennaisance* (London, 1972), pp. 110-111.

and excitement engendered by his work would set in motion a chain of events culminating in the triumph of Kitty Hawk in 1903.[5]

Other experimenters who followed in Cayley's wake during the first half of the 19th century, notably the Englishmen William Henson and John Stringfellow, made few technical contributions to aeronautics, but did popularize the subject and cement the modern configuration of the airplane in the public consciousness. While the flying machine became a bit more plausible, the absence of an organized drive toward the final goal continued to retard researchers. The professional technicians who took up the cause of the flying machine after 1860 supplied the coordination and direction that gave birth to such a drive.[6]

The industrial revolution of the 18th century had forced a redefinition of mankind's relationship to the machine. The development of new machines, processes and technical solutions to the economic and social problems that plagued an increasingly urban, regimented, and factory-oriented society could no longer be trusted to a class of ingenious mechanics. A new order of the men who made their living by technology was in the offing. A hierarchy of technicians, ranging from the applied scientist through various grades of mechanic and engineer, replaced the traditional hand methods of the guild craftsman. While self-trained technicians, like Eli Whitney, S. F. B. Morse, Samuel Colt, and Charles Goodyear, continued to inject new ideas, techniques, and machines into industry, the leadership that directed the sustained growth of modern technology was drawn from an expanding pool of trained engineers.

With the passage of time these men developed a self-conscious desire for recognition as professionals. Endowed with esoteric knowledge by virtue of specialized training, they were proud of the links that had been forged between science and technology, and were cognizant of new responsibilities to put their training and abilities to use for the benefit of all mankind.

In their drive to achieve professional status, engineers borrowed the analytical methods and problem-solving techniques that had proven valuable in science. In addition, they adapted the social, institutional and organizational structures of the scientific community. As Edwin Layton has demonstrated, 19th century technology was establishing a "mirror image" relationship with science. The goals differed, but the methods and internal structure of the two pursuits were drawing ever close.[7]

As one difficult problem after another fell before the onslaught of the new

5. For the career of Sir George Cayley see: J. L. Pritchard, *Sir George Cayley: The Inventor of the Airplane* (London, 1960); C. H. Gibbs-Smith, *Sir George Cayley's Aeronautics, 1796-1855* (London, 1962).

6. M. J. B. Davy, *Henson and Stringfellow: Their Work in Aeronautics* (London, 1931).

7. Edwin Layton, "Mirror Image Twins: The Communities of Science and Technology in Nineteenth Century America," *Technology and Culture,* 12 (October 1971), pp. 562-580. For the general development of the engineering profession see: W. H. G. Armytage, *A Social History of Engineering* (New York, 1961).

technology, engineers were to develop an almost boundless self-confidence in their abilities. They sought new challenges, new areas in which to demonstrate their prowess. The airplane furnished one of the most difficult of these challenges.

Engineers were prepared by training and experience to treat the flying machine in the same manner as any other mechanical problem. Many discovered that elements of their professional experience could be applied directly to aeronautics. Octave Chanute, an American civil engineer, became interested in aviation when he recognized that his understanding of bridge analysis and locomotive air resistance could be used to explain aerodynamic phenomena. Robert Thurston, an American pioneer in the field of strength of materials, became particularly interested in the most useful construction materials for a flying machine. The central point is clear. By 1860 a significant number of key engineers were willing to consider the problem of flight as amenable to solution as any other that had been overcome by the application of their developing professional methodology.

During the last half of the century, a sense of community became a major element directing the course of action for engineers involved in aeronautics. This cooperative ideal was expressed through both formal and informal organizations of professional technologists. Membership in professional societies was a familiar experience to engineers by 1870. The foundation of such groups had been one indication of the fact that engineers were attempting to establish themselves as distinct, useful and highly trained professionals.

Engineers interested in the flying machine simply transferred the system of professional communication and information sharing to which they were accustomed in their normal engineering pursuits to the study of aeronautics. Sir George Cayley had attempted to interest other amateur experimenters in founding an aeronautical society in 1816, 1837, and 1840, but without success. The first such groups, the *Société Aérostatique et Métérologique*, founded in Paris in 1852, and the *Société d'Autolocomotion Aérienne*, established in 1862 emphasized the development of lighter-than-air machines. Thus, the Aeronautical Society of Great Britain, founded in 1866, was the first engineering organization to exhibit a serious interest in the airplane.

The Aeronautical Society drew some distinguished amateur experimenters into membership during its early years, but professional engineers provided much of the guidance and leadership for the group. Francis Herbert Wenham, a well-known marine engineer and engine designer; Charles Brooke, a designer of self-recording instruments; Sir William Fairbain, one-time president of both the Institution of Science and the British Association for the Advancement of Science; Sir Charles Bright, a planner and supporter of the Atlantic cable; W. H. le Feuvre, president of the Society of Engineers; and Sir Charles William Siemans, a pioneer developer of both the telegraph and dynamo — were among the prominent technicians who served on the Council or ruling body of the Society during the first two years of its existance. These men were not figureheads; they played active roles in directing the course of the organization.

Other leading engineers who served on society technical committees or offered papers at early meetings included James Nasmyth, the inventor of the steam hammer; Thomas Moy, an associate of the Institute of Naval Architects and the owner of a small engineering firm that specialized in the manufacture of steam engines and boilers; J. P. Bourne of the Institution of Civil Engineers; F. W. Young, an engineer with the Harbours and Rivers Division of the Colonial Service, and Mr. A. Alexander, manager of the Camel Steel Works at Sheffield. While the total membership of the society numbered only 65 at the end of 1867, some of the finest engineers in England were enthusiastic participants in its activities.[8]

In addition to sponsoring a series of lectures, the Aeronautical Society was responsible for the first public exhibition of aeronautical technology.

The *Annual Reports* of the Aeronautical Society proved to be the organization's most useful venture. For many years after the issue of the first volume this series remained the primary source of trustworthy information on aeronautics. The quality of the articles published in the *Annual Reports* was consistently high. The publication was aimed at a professional audience of scientists and engineers, not the lay public. The common denominator connecting most of the articles appearing in the series was the attempt to extend contemporary engineering theory and practice into aeronautics. The authors of these pieces were not foolish dreamers or visionaries, but working engineers who perceived aviation as a solvable problem.

European engineers also followed the English lead in establishing aeronautical journals aimed at a professional audience. *L'Aéronaut,* which began publication in Paris in 1869, was followed by *Revue de l'Aéronautique,* founded in 1888. German engineers also developed aeronautical journals during the two decades after 1860.

By 1875, then, European engineers interested in aeronautics had publicly announced their belief in the possibility of flight. They had banded together in aeronautical societies designed to advance the cause of the flying machine. Moreover, a small number of technical journals had appeared that treated the subject of aviation in a manner intended to appeal to fellow professionals. The study of aeronautics was well on its way to respectability as an acceptable field of research for engineers.

The immediate effect was to encourage a dialogue that enabled technical professionals to fix known points of reference. A foundation of basic data that could serve as a starting point for active experimentation was prepared as the first step toward the development of a successful heavier-than-air flying machine.

As scattered engineers began the task of translating the data accumulated

8. *Annual Reports of the Aeronautical Society of Great Britain,* 1868-1888, *passim*; J. L. Pritchard, "The Royal Aeronautical Society: The First Fifty Years—1866 and All That," *Journal of the Royal Aeronautical Society* (March-July 1961).

in their newly established journals into an operating airplane, the basic dimensions of the task emerged. It was clear that a completed flying machine would represent the successful amalgamation of solutions to problems in the basic areas of aircraft structures, aerodynamics and power plant and propeller technology.

The technology of aircraft structures—the choice of materials and assembly techniques to be used in building a safe airframe—was the least critical of these three areas. Most experimenters chose to employ standard materials whose properties were thoroughly understood. Nor was innovation in construction technology encouraged. Procedures long accepted as standard in carpentry and the building trades were to prevail in aeronautics as well. Civil engineering contributed basic data on trussing systems, strength of materials, and the properties of various structural forms under stress, but for the most part, structural problems were solved empirically.

Would-be flying machine builders paid a great deal more attention to propulsion technology. Attitudes toward the engine problem varied between two extremes. One group of experimenters saw the development of a suitable power plant as the single most important difficulty. These men dedicated their efforts to the perfection of the ideal aero engine and tended to move to the construction of full size machines or test beds based on minimum aerodynamic research. Others believed that once the far more difficult aerodynamic problems had been overcome, a suitable engine would be relatively easy to obtain.

The choice of power plant varied. Steam was the obvious early candidate. As late as the last decade of the 19th century, S. P. Langley, James Means, Octave Chanute, Hiram Maxim and Clement Ader would continue to counsel that the enormous body of experience with light weight steam engines and boilers made them the logical choice for an experimental aero power plant.

The potential of the internal combustion engine was more difficult to recognize. Prior to 1895, most serious experimenters were forced to conclude that the new engine technology was simply too experimental and unreliable for use in a life or death flight situation. There was an additional, though unrecognized, danger in the gasoline engine. As S. P. Langley was to discover, the experimenter who braved the relative unknowns of the lightweight petrol engine in addition to developing an airplane, added years to his search and needlessly compounded his problems. The ability of the Wright brothers to design and build a primitive gasoline engine with relative ease would have been impossible a decade earlier.

Finally, a few enthusiasts focused on extremely lightweight power plants suitable for brief periods of operation. Compressed air and carbonic acid gas engines were the most common choices in this category, particularly with model builders of those who chose to take to the skies in very light proto-airplanes that were essentially powered hang gliders.

By the last quarter of the 19th century much thought was also being given to the means of translating the power of the engine into forward motion. The oars, sails, flapping wings and paddle wheels of an earlier epoch had almost universally given way to the propeller. Few enthusiasts were willing to invest time and energy in studies of propeller efficiency, however. Thus, the inadequate conception of the "air screw" boring through air was retained until overthrown by the brilliant Wright treatment of the propeller as a rotary wing generating a forward lift vector.

It was in the area of aerodynamics that the first generation of engineers in aeronautics made their most significant contributions. The design of a proper wing was obviously the central concern. Cayley had demonstrated that the whirling arm, ballastic pendulums and other insturments devised by the 18th century ballisticians could provide general data of value in guiding flying machine builders. The development of new instruments, most notably the wind tunnel, introduced by F. H. Wenham and John Browning in 1871, was to prove far more important, however, for it opened entirely new approaches to the study of aerodynamic phenomena underlying wing design.

In many respects Wenham can be seen as the prototype of the investigators who would achieve the success of 1903. He advocated the construction of gliding machines with which a pilot could gain experience in the air prior to adding an engine. Such machines were to be thoroughly grounded in engineering data obtained by means of the most advanced experimental apparatus. His use of the wind tunnel, for example, directly inspired the Wright brothers' later application of this device.[9]

The wind tunnel made it possible to estimate the wing surface area required to support a given weight. As this minimum area began to appear too large to deal with as a single wing, Wenham suggested the use of multiple surfaces. Biplane, triplane, multiplane, and tandem wing configurations made their appearance in the plans of the most realistic experimenters. Only in this manner could the needed surface area be embodied in a machine that would remain reasonably small, light and manuverable.

Attention was also focused on the correct shape for a wing. Cayley had tentatively suggested that an arched surface was more efficient than a flat plane, but it remained for professional technicians to firmly establish the virtue of the cambered wing after 1860. Wenham initiated this process by arguing that all bird wings were arched. He also noted that the center of maximum pressure fell toward the thick leading edge. This belief helps to explain Wenham's choice of long, narrow (high aspect ratio) multiplane wings for his own gliders of 1858-1859.

Horatio F. Phillips, following Wenham's lead, turned his own ingenious steam injection wind tunnel to the study of cambered air foils. The surfaces that emerged from these tests represent an important step toward the modern airfoil. Phillips emphasized the two-surface wing section in which the upper side of the airfoil was given a gentler curve than the bottom side. This,

9. J. L. Pritchard, "Francis Herbert Wenham, Honorary Members, 1824-1908: An Appreciation of the First Lecturer to the Aeronautical Society," *Journal of the Royal Aeronautical Society*, 62 (August 1958), pp. 571-596.

in combination within leading and trailing edges rising to maximum thickness near the supposed center of pressure, one-third to one-half the distance behind the leading edge, resulted in several sections with a distinctly modern appearance. Phillips applied his wing theory in the construction of a multiplane slat wing test bed that was capable of short tethered hops from a circular track.[10]

With work underway on the development of an effective wing, attention turned to the other great aerodynamic problem — control. As in the case of powerplant research, attitudes toward stability and control varied widely.

Unlike a vehicle operating on land or water, an aircraft in flight is free to rotate about three axes of motion. The craft can "pitch" its nose up or down to initiate a climb or descent, or "yaw" its nose to the right or left in a flat turn in one plane. The third, or "roll," axis is employed when the machine, by raising one wingtip and lowering the other, rotates about an imaginary line drawn through the center of the fuselage.

The implements for controlling motion in yaw and pitch, had appeared long before 1860. Eighteenth century balloonists had suggested the adaptation of the ship's rudder for steering their proposed aerial craft. It was but a short step to a "horizontal rudder," or elevator that could be employed to regulate altitude. In his basic glider model of 1804, Cayley had used a cruciform tail that combined rudder and elevator.

Control in roll (lateral control) was quite another matter, for no analogy like a ship's rudder could be drawn from older technologies. A search of the 19th century patent records and the aeronautical literature does indicate that a few imaginative men were giving thought to the problem, but those few suggestions for roll control attracted little or no comment. Almost invariably, the men who actively sought to take to the skies before 1903 failed to recognize a need for active lateral control. Many of them, in fact, denied the need for effective pilot control in any axis except pitch. Following the lead of the French experimenter Alphonse Penaud, they sought to perfect a mechanism that could guarantee absolute inherent stability. This would mean a flying machine would proceed on a straight and level course, with the pilot intervening only when a change in direction or altitude was required. Thus, a simple mechanism such as building dihedral into the wings, which would provide some measure of stability in roll, was substituted for an active control system. The rudder alone would be used to swing the aircraft around in a slow flat turn.

A number of factors combine to explain this emphasis on automatic stability. A great many students of the atmosphere were convinced that upper air gusts and currents shifted so rapidly as to defeat human reflexes. They

10. C. H. Gibbs-Smith, *Aviation: An Historical Survey From its Origins to the End of World War II*, (London, 1970), pp. 53-54. For other information on the birth of aerodynamics see J. L. Pritchard, "The Dawn of Aerodynamics," *Journal of the Royal Aeronautical Society*, 61 (March 1957), p. 151 and Theodore von Kármán, *Aerodynamics: Selected Topics in the Light of Their Historical Development*. (Ithaca, 1954).

believed that a mechanism that could "sense" these changes and automatically maintain the craft on an even keel was required.

Just as important, however, is the fact that few experimenters really sought
to develop a finished aircraft, complete with adequate controls. Most felt that
the first task was to demonstrate a simple straight-line flight with a man on
board. Once this had been accomplished, they argued, full attention could be
given to control.

As Charles H. Gibbs-Smith has pointed out, 19th century flying machine
builders may be broadly categorized as "chauffeurs" or "airmen" with regard
to their control philosophies. The "chauffeurs" assumed that an airplane
could be operated as though it were a vehicle running on a flat surface, while
the airmen sought to master the motion of their craft in the new medium. The
fact remained, however, that as long as even the "airmen" pursued the chim-
era of automatic stability, or resorted to acrobatic body movements to control
their craft, progress toward a genuine airplane would be severely limited.[11]

At any rate, it is clear that by 1875, only a decade after the large scale entry
of engineers into aeronautics, profound changes had occurred in flgiht
studies. The boundaries of the problem were being mapped. The appearance
of an organized dialogue among men trained to attack any technical problem
with powerful analytical tools had prepared the ground for active flight researchers. Flying machines produced by inventors in the mainstream of
aeronautics would no longer be the product of a single mind working in
isolation. To a greater or lesser extent they would represent a distillation of
the experience of other professionals in the field. Aeronautics was on its way
to elevation as an engineering discipline.

The next step was obvious. This influx of new data would be translated into
an operating flying machine.

Three basic practical approaches to the development of the airplane
emerged. Some experimenters chose to forge ahead to the construction of full
scale machines with few intermediate steps. Confident that all aerodynamic
problems could be solved on paper, they concentrated their attention on the
development of a suitable aeronautical power plant.

Hiram Maxim was the best known of these figures. An expatriated American living in England, Maxim developed what amounted to an enormous
engine test bed designed to operate on an 1,800 foot runway. Trials of the craft
in 1892 and 1893 were marred by accidents and breakage, culminating in the
end of the tests when the craft, which was held in place by an upper rail, rose
slightly and was smashed.[12]

Clement Ader, a French pioneer of the telephone, also chose to construct a
full scale machine with little previous model or glider testing. His *Eole* of 1890
made a short uncontrolled powered hop, while his *Avion III* of 1897 refused to

11. Gibbs-Smith, *Aviation*, pp. 58-59.

12. For detailed contemporary citations for all figures discussed see: Paul Brockett, *A Bibliography of Aeronautics* (Washington, 1910); For Maxim see Hiram Maxim, *Artificial and Natural
Flight* (New York, 1908); Hiram Maxim, "The Aeroplane," *Cosmopolitan*, 13 (June 1892), p. 205.

leave the ground. In both cases the all important problem of control had been given almost no attention. This approach to the problem of flight was naive, and while Maxim and Ader aroused considerable interest and generated much publicity, they contributed nothing to the progress of flight technology.[13]

A second experimental tradition that evolved during the latter half of the 19th century called for the use of model aircraft to investigate flight problems. Surely, these men reasoned, if an efficient large powered model could be flown, then the creation of man-carrying craft would involve nothing more than "scaling-up" the original. Models seemed ideal. Being small, they would be reasonably inexpensive; could be flown repeatedly; and did not risk a pilot's life.

Sir George Cayley had first pointed to the utility of the model with his classic glider of 1804. Between 1850 and 1875 a number of enthusiasts, including Felix du Temple, Gustave Trouvé, Victor Tatin, and Thomas Moy succeeded in producing at least tentative flights with models powered by clockwork mechanisms, compressed air and steam engines.

The most influential model maker of the period, however, was Alphonse Penaud, a French marine engineer who introduced the use of twisted rubber strands as a model power plant. Penaud, who was active during the decade of the 1870's, was also the first to construct a model embodying a useful degree of inherent stability, an absolute necessity for any pilotless aircraft.

Lawrence Hargrave, the Australian pioneer, while not basically a modeler, is definitely a member of this group. Hargrave, who did build and fly several very interesting models, is perhaps best known as the inventor of the box-kite. Like Penaud, he was much interested in problems of automatic stability.[14]

The full scale glider provided the most popular approach to the flying machine problem. Cayley and Wenham had pioneered in this field. Wenham's high aspect ratio multiplane of 1858-59 in which the pilot lay prone was, technically, one of the most influential designs of the entire pre-Wright epoch. The South African John Household, the French-Egyptian experimenter Louis Mouillard, and the American John Joseph Montgomery were also active in building and flying hang gliders before 1890.[15]

Otto Lilienthal was, without doubt, the most influential of the gliding pioneers. Born in Anklam, Pomerania, Lilienthal was trained as a mechanical engineer. His interest in flight dated to his boyhood, but he did not undertake a serious study of the problems involved until 1879, when he

---

13. C. H. Gibbs-Smith, *Clement Ader: His Flight Claims and His Place in History* (London, 1968).

14. For all figures above see C. H. Gibbs-Smith, *Aviation, passim;* and C. H. Gibbs-Smith, *The Invention of the Aeroplane* (London, 1965), *passim.*

15. Hannes Oberhalzer, *Pioneers of Early Aviation in South Africa.* (Bloemfontein, 1974), pp. 7-11; A. D. Spearman, *John Joseph Montgomery, 1858-1911: Father of Basic Flying* (Santa Clara, 1967).

began a series of experiments in aerodynamics that produced the most trustworthy air pressure data available at that time. He began work on the hang gliders that were to spread his fame around the globe in 1892. During the next four years he would develop 18 distinct glider types, including both monoplanes and biplanes.

There can be no doubt that Lilienthal's phenomenal success was the greatest single factor in building popular enthusiasm for aeronautics. Photos showing his craft skimming effortlessly through the air were published in newspapers and magazines in Europe and America. He was the "flying man," the "winged Prussian," the "German Darius Green." These articles and photos were of enormous significance, for they convinced all but the most adamant skeptics that heavier-than-air flight was possible for man. His work was to inspire others, including Wilbur and Orville Wright, to try their own hand at gliding.

Even in death Lilienthal had a major impact on the growth of aeronautics. He succumbed to injuries suffered in a glider crash on August 9, 1896, the first martyr to the cause of the aeroplane.[16]

Percy S. Pilcher, Lilienthal's chief European disciple, also built and flew hang gliders. Like his German mentor, Pilcher died in a glider crash in 1899.[17]

These early pioneers had forged new paths based on the work of the engineers. None, however, was able to carry his work to its logical conclusion. While models were flown, no experimenter attempted to scale up his craft to man-carrying dimensions, nor were any of the glider builders successful in adding power plants to their machines. Men had taken tentatively to the air, but an obvious plateau had been reached far short of complete success.

Geographic isolation, a lack of close immediate communication, and personal rivalry and jealousy were the principal retarding factors. James Means, an American aeronautical enthusiast and publisher of the influential *Aeronautical Annual*, commented on this situation:

"Maxim speaks of Lilienthal as a parachutist, and likens him to a flying squirrel . . . Lilienthal, after alluding to the unwieldiness of Maxim's machine, says, 'After all, the result of his labors has been to show us how not to do it.' If any two men should be friends rather than foes, these are the two. Each has certain ideas and publications which the other lacks and it is the greatest of pities that they cannot clasp hands over the watery channel."[18]

These final difficulties were to be overcome as leadership in the search for a successful airplane passed to the United States. American engineers had watched with interest as their fellow professionals in Europe began work in aeronautics. By 1890, a unique community composed of American techni-

16. Gerhard Halle, *Otto Lilienthal* (Dusseldorf, 1956); Gerhard Halle, *Otto Lilienthal und seine Flugzeug-Hanstructionen* (Munich, 1962); Werner Schwipps, *Otto Lilienthals Flugversuche* (Berlin, 1966).

17. Percy Pilcher, "Gliding Experiments," *Aeronautical Annual*, 3 (Boston, 1897), p. 144.

18. James Means, "An Editorial," *Aeronautical Annual*, 1 (Boston, 1894), p. 2.

cians involved in flying machine studies had evolved. Unlike the formal organizations that had appeared in Europe, the American aeronautical community can best be defined as a loose network of professional technicians interested in the problems of flight. The activity of the community was focused in a number of major research centers in Boston, Washington, D. C., and Chicago. Smaller packets of interest were scattered from Fallmouth, Maine, to Santa Clara, California. Each of these centers pursued its own approach to flight, yet all were bound by common needs and interests into a functioning unit. Extended correspondence and personal visits, the exchange of personnel, and joint participation in flying trials, seminars and symposia were all factors that worked to create a research environment unlike any the world of aeronautics had seen before.[19]

Octave Chanute was the driving force behind the rise of this community of experimenters. Born in Paris in 1832, Chanute had emigrated to the United States at the age of six with his parents. Determined to become a civil engineer, he began work as the humblest member of a railroad surveying crew. Within a few years, he had worked his way up through the ranks to the position of chief engineer with a number of western rail lines. He reached the pinnacle of his career when he was named chief engineer of the reorganized Erie Railroad in 1875. In addition, he had been awarded a number of impressive engineering contracts for major structures, including the first bridge over the Missouri River at St. Charles, and the Chicago Stock Yards.

Chanute became interested in aeronautics in 1875, and began corresponding with major aeronautical figures around the world. He was quickly recognized as an international clearing house for information on aviation. The publication of this accumulated data, initially in a series of articles and eventually in the classic volume of 1891, *Progress in Flying Machines*, firmly established his reputation as the authority on the state of aeronautical science.

By the 1880's Chanute had launched a campaign to interest American engineers in flight. He lectured to local engineering groups, engineering students in colleges, and arranged aeronautical sessions for major national meetings of organizations, like the American Association for the Advancement of Science. This period of activity was to culminate in the International Conference on Aerial Navigation held at Chicago in 1893. Chanute's effort resulted in the creation of a genuine and widespread interest in aviation among engineers in the U. S. As had been the case in Europe, some of the most prominent names in American engineering became active or passive supporters of the flying machine effort.

Samuel Pierpont Langley, another primary focus of the American aeronaut-

19. Tom D. Crouch, *"To Ride The Fractious Horse; The American Aeronautical Community and the Problem of Heavier-Than-Air Flight, 1875-1905.* (Unpublished Ph.D. Dissertation, The Ohio State University, 1976); Tom D. Crouch, "Americans and the Airplane, 1875-1903" *Aviation Quarterly,* 2-3 (Winter 1976-Winter 1977), *passim,* are the sources for all material on the activity and personalities of the American aeronautical community not otherwise cited.

ical community, was one of those attracted to flight by Chanute's enthusiasm. A self-trained astronomer, Langley was highly regarded as a
pioneer researcher in astrophysics. As Secretary of the Smithsonian Institution, he had built a solid reputation as an administrator of science.

Langley's infatuation with the flying machine began when he attended a
lecture on aeronautics organized by Chanute at the Buffalo meeting of the
American Association for the Advancement of Science in 1885. He left the
meeting inspired to prove or disprove the possibility of flight. Beginning with
an experimental study of the physical principles underlying flight, he became
convinced that it was not only possible for men to fly, but, that the goals
would, in fact, be easier to achieve than anyone had previously thought
possible.

In an effort to provide a practical demonstration of his conclusions, Langley
constructed a series of rubber-powered models, all of which failed to meet his
expectations. Dissatisfied, he began work on what would eventually become
seven large steam-powered "aerodromes" with wingspans of up to fourteen
feet. The construction of these machines forced Langley to devote large
amounts of Smithsonian time, money, and personnel to a concentrated
model development effort. This search procedure was very much goal-
oriented and empirical. There was little concern for the niceties of aerodynamics. Rather, all attention was focused on immediate problems, including
the creation of a structure that was just strong enough to accept flight
stresses, and a power plant that would keep the craft in the air for an
appreciable period. Success finally came in the spring and fall of 1896, when
two of the jewel-like aerodromes made unequivocal flights under their own
power.[20]

1896 was a key year for the developing aeronautical community in the
United States. In addition to Langley's triumph, Octave Chanute and four
companions had camped on the dunes ringing the Indiana shore of Lake
Michigan for flight tests with a number of manned gliders. One of these craft,
a biplane designed by Chanute and his associate, A. M. Herring, represented
a significant step away from the more primitive Lilienthal hang glider.[21]

Interest in flight was on the rise in other parts of the nation as well. A third
major focus of interest developed in Boston, where James Means, Samuel
Cabot, A. A. Merrill and others organized the Boston Aeronautical Society in
1895. This group was to serve a major communications function. Means's
Aeronautical Annuals published between 1895 and 1897 were the most
important new serial publications in aeronautics since the *Annual Reports of
The Aeronautical Society of Great Britain* had first appeared a quarter century earlier. In addition, Means was extraordinarily successful in encourag-
ing major American newspaper and magazine editors to open their columns
to a discussion of aviation issues. Means and other members of the Boston

20. S. P. Langley *Memoir on Mechanical Flight* (Washington, 1911).

21. Octave Chanute, "Recent Experiments in Gliding Flight," *Aeronautical Annual*, 3 (Boston,
1897).

circle also played an influential role in the informal communications network that bound American experimenters.

Single individuals and small groups all over the United States had entered the life of the community by 1896. A. F. Zahm of Notre Dame and Catholic University was establishing the first large scale American wind tunnel and providing advice and assistance to a wide range of experimenters. In Schenectady, Charles Proteus Steinmetz and the members of the first American glider club, the Mohawk Aerial Navigators, were trying—without much success—to get into the air. C. H. Larson in Maine was flying his Lilienthal glider and planning a series of large manlifting kites. By 1898 Edson F. Gallaudet, coach of the Yale crew and an instructor in the physics department, would be hard at work on an extremely interesting wing warping model designed to be flown as a kite.

Nor had the heroes of American invention ignored the airplane. John Holland filled the nation's newspapers and magazines with his flight schemes, while Thomas Alva Edison was regaling interviewers with his vision of future aerial craft. Alexander Graham Bell, an old friend of Samuel Langley, and an official witness of the 1896 aerodrome flights, was soon hard at work on his own aerodrome kites. Charles Duryea, the American automotive pioneer, was counseling young engineers to take to the air in gliders, "Flying is within our grasp; we have naught to do but take it."[22]

The American aeronautical community was in full operation by the mid-90's. In Chicago and Boston those experimenters regarded as most promising were able to find full time work in aeronautics. Octave Chanute was not only employing select men to build and test his own designs, but was offering generous support for the work of others both in the United States and abroad. In still other cases, he attempted to create syndicates to back the experiments of inventors like Maxim and Mouillard. S. P. Langley was employing a small number of engineers on the aerodrome program. In addition, he made small sums of Hodgkins Fund grant money available to select individuals.

The movement of employees from one group to another is an indication of the extent to which the community was successful in channeling effort. A. M. Herring, a product of the mechanical engineering program at the Stevens Institute of Technology, had begun building kites and powered models, as well as flying full scale copies of Lilienthal gliders, as early as 1894. He went to work for Chanute in 1895 building models intended to develop a configuration for a new glider type. Late in 1895, James Means brought Herring's work to the attention of Langley who, after consultation with Chanute, hired the young man to superintend work on the aerodromes. Herring returned to Chanute's employ in 1896 and participated in the Lake Michigan glider trials, then found another sponsor to support his work on an additional glider and, in 1898, a powered hang glider that made two short hops from a beach at St. Joseph, Michigan. In 1902, Chanute hired him once again to build a new

22. C. F. Duryea, "Learning How to Fly," in *Proceedings of the International Conference on Aerial Navigation* (New York, 1894).

glider and paid Herring's expenses while he lived in the Wright camp at Kitty Hawk.

The career of E. C. Huffaker, a Tennessee native with an M.S. in engineering from the University of Virginia, followed a similar, if less complex, course. Charles M. Manly, a graduate engineer from Cornell's Sibley College provides a further illustration of the way in which the community worked to draw the most able men into flight research. Manly was a student of Robert H. Thurston, who was a close friend of Chanute's and a participant in the activities of the community. Chanute, at Thurston's invitation, had lectured on aeronautics at Cornell and drawn an enthusiastic response from the student engineers, including young Manly. In 1898, when Langley was looking for a bright graduate engineer to supervise the construction and testing of the full scale aerodrome, it was only natural that he should turn to Thurston for suggestions, and thus learn of Manly.

Conditions for progress in aeronautics were now ideal, and it was in America that the work of the earlier European experimenters was carried to fruition. Langley was able to realize the dream of the modelers as he scaled-up the successful 1896 aerodromes to man carrying dimensions. Funded by the U.S. Army Board of Ordnance and Fortification as well as miscellaneous Smithsonian monies, Aerodrome A, the "Great Aerodrome," was the result of a five year development program. Langley believed that the production of the airframe presented few difficulties, for the lessons learned in the construction of the models were applied in the full scale craft. Every attempt was made to duplicate other conditions that had led to success in 1896 as well. The catapult launch from a houseboat was retained, as was the simple control system. A cruciform tail served as an elevator while a large rudder was placed on the underside of the machine. Lateral stability was supplied by the marked dihedral of the wings.

The creation of an internal combustion engine to power the Great Aerodrome presented a great many more difficulties, however. When Stephan Balzer, the original engine contractor, failed to obtain anything close to the required power, Manly took over the task, eventually producing a superb radial piston engine.[23]

The failure of the Great Aerodrome illustrated the weaknesses inherent in the modeling tradition. Langley's desire to adhere to his experience with the smaller craft ensured the development of a full-scale machine that was structurally weak, virtually uncontrollable, and burdened with a launch system that imposed disastrous structural loads before a flight began.

The most advanced end product of the Chanute research, the Herring powered hang glider of 1898, points to a similar failure of vision. Like Lilienthal and Pilcher, Herring saw a hang glider powered by an ultra-light-weight engine as a necessary intermediate step before attempting work on a complete airplane. In striving to solve this simpler problem, these men had

23. Robert Meyer, *The Langley Aero Engine of 1903* (Washington, 1971).

severely retarded their own work toward the ultimate goal. They continued to work with the necessarily small gliders that could be controlled by body shifting, thus ignoring the one major problem that still required solution, the creation of an effective mechanism to provide three axis control.

The airplane had remained an elusive goal in 1900, and the experiments conducted by the members of the American aeronautical community had failed. Nevertheless, the group had expanded the bounds of aeronautical knowledge, and had proven enormously successful in creating precisely those social and intellectual conditions that made progress possible.

The Wrights deserve full credit for the final brilliant breakthroughs that led to the triumph at Kitty Hawk, yet they owed a major debt to the engineering tradition and the community of aeronautical enthusiasts that had helped shape the course of their work. Only eight years separate the Wrights' entry into aeronautics from the first flight of the 1903 airplane. The first three crucial years of this period were entirely devoted to a detailed study of the four decades of engineering experience that had accumulated in the aeronautical literature. The ability to draw maximum benefit from the lessons of the past was one of the early marks of the Wright genius.

It was also during this period that the brothers made their first direct contact with the leaders of American flight research. They sought the advice of Samuel Langley. Octave Chanute became their closest associate in aeronautics and a constant source of encouragement and advice. It was Chanute who spread word of the Wright success.

Their assessment of the total body of experience provided the baseline for their own experimental program. Their approach, active gliding, was in the tradition of Cayley, Wenham, Lilienthal, and Chanute. The basic configuration of the early Wright gliders was a derivation of the Wenham multiplane and Chanute biplane designs. Their initial work relied on Lilienthal air pressure tables, as transmitted by Chanute. When these tables proved inaccurate, they turned to the wind tunnel, pioneered by Wenham and Phillips. In later years they were to express their gratitude to Lilienthal with a gift of $1,000 to his widow.

Thus, Wilbur and Orville Wright emerged directly from the research tradition established by professional technicians in aeronautics. Their own talents enabled them to move far beyond their predecessors, yet they had not begun work with a blank slate. Their own brilliant success rested on an institutional structure that had been prepared by two generations of engineers in aeronautics.

TOM D. CROUCH, Curator of Astronautics with the National Air and Space Museum, is a native of Dayton, Ohio. He received his Ph.D. in history from Ohio State University in 1976. He is the author of *The Giant Leap: A Chronology of Ohio Aerospace Events and Personalities, 1815-1969* (Columbus, 1971). He edited *Charles A. Lindbergh: An American Life* (Washington, 1977), and has published a number of other articles on aspects of aerospace history. Dr. Crouch was the 1976 recipient of the History Manuscript Award of the American Institute of Aeronautics and Astronautics. He has been named AIAA Distinguished Lecturer for 1978.

Wilbur and Orville Wright: Seventy-Five Years After

MARVIN W. McFARLAND

Seventy-five years ago, on December 14, 1903, the Wrights made the first trial of their power machine at Kill Devil Hills, North Carolina. Wilbur won the toss of the coin and got the first turn. It was an abortive flight, the track being laid down the hill, and the pilot made an error of judgment at the start. Nevertheless, the airplane traveled one hundred twelve feet and the power and control were proved ample. The telegram the boys sent their father, Bishop Milton Wright, the next day ended with the words: "Success assured, Keep quiet."

"Success assured." How characteristic of the Wrights! Their confidence in final success was unbounded. It is this that stands out about them seventy-five years later.

Charles Harvard Gibbs-Smith has very kindly called me the dean of American Wright scholars. If I am, I am the first to confess that I got into the Wright business purely by accident. While I was still a humble peon in the office of General Carl Spaatz, the first Chief of Staff of the U.S. Air Force, Orville Wright died in his seventy-seventh year, on January 30, 1948. His elder brother Wilbur had died thirty-six years earlier, on May 30, 1912. Before the year 1948 was out I had moved from the Air Force to the Library of Congress. The Wright papers were received in the Library on May 27, 1949, as the result of a decision — which Orville Wright had authorized in his will — made by Harold S. Miller and Harold W. Steeper, co-executors of the estate.

Part of the commitment regarding the gift was an agreement by the Library to publish such of the papers as contained the record of the Wrights' invention of the airplane. The job of studying the collection with a view to publication was assigned to me in the late spring of 1950, and a year later I recommended not a series of brochures, as was originally proposed, but a full edition of all the pertinent material. The proposal was accepted and I got the job. When the Wright family learned that someone named McFarland was going to edit the papers, they were dismayed. There was a McFarland they knew and distrusted, and they were afraid that he had gotten the task. They were relieved to find out that the actual editor was young and unknown, a person who had never met Wilbur or Orville Wright and had no ax to grind. So that is why I am invited to write this paper. I must state that I have done nothing significant about the Wrights for many years. There are others who are much more current Wright scholars than I am. I will not therefore forecast or speculate about the future, but rather remind and admonish, which is essentially the function of one who looks back.

First, I should like to emphasize, as Stanton is supposed to have said of Lincoln, that the Wrights belong to the ages. Anybody is free to say anything about them that he or she likes, providing there is responsibility for the statement. What follow are therefore my own views, in no way to be interpreted as the party line. What I say is stated entirely on my own volition and on my own authority.

The Wrights began to study the problem of flight deliberately. That is not to say that they were not fascinated by other matters; they were. But they looked around rather cold-bloodedly for something they could sink their teeth into and bring to completion or near-completion. The steamship and the use of metal in constructing ships were accomplished facts. The submarine had been invented. Trains of cars were drawn at speed by steam locomotives on steel rails. The electric light and the telephone were realities. Talking machines with megaphone speakers graced many homes. Wireless telegraphy was in being. The automobile was an increasingly popular and efficient means of transportation, and the improved bicycle produced a craze to which they themselves had succumbed. New rifled guns, cannon, and trinitrotoluene — TNT — were making big war thinkable if not inevitable. The balloon, though not yet the dirigible, had proven its use for conveying messages, some in microform. The modern world was essentially in place. Virtually only the heavier-than-air flying machine remained an unsolved — and some said an insoluble — problem. To unravel this enigma was grist for the Wrights' mill.

The Wrights never claimed to be going at the thing *ab initio.* They made no such pretension. Many aspects of the problem were solved; many others were believed solved. Wilbur, the natural but self-appointed spokesman of the duo, wrote on May 30, 1899, to the Smithsonian Institution:

> " . . . I am an enthusiast, but not a crank in the sense that I have some pet theories as to the proper construction of a flying machine. I wish to avail myself of all that is already known and then if possible add my mite to help on the future worker who will attain final success . . . "

With less naiveté Wilbur wrote his father on September 3, 1900, on the eve of departing for Kitty Hawk for the first time:

> " . . . It is my belief that flight is possible and while I am taking up the investigation for pleasure rather than profit, I think there is a slight chance of achieving fame and fortune from it. It is almost the only great problem which has not been pursued by a multitude of investigators, and therefore carried to a point where further progress is very difficult. I

am certain I can reach a point much in advance of any previous workers in this field even if complete success is not attained at present . . . ."

That the Wrights were tinkerers, bicycle mechanics who struck it lucky and built an airplane that flew, are charges it is painful to have brought against them seventy-five years later. It is little short of disgraceful that anyone anywhere in the world can entertain such nonsensical thoughts today.

Atop the Big Kill Devil Hill stands the Wright Memorial monument, erected by the American people during the lifetime of Orville Wright, the only instance of a national monument being put up while one of the persons to whom it is dedicated was still alive. National monuments do not memorialize tinkerers, however clever. Around the pylon are inscribed the words:

> "In commemoration of the conquest of the air by the brothers Wilbur and Orville Wright. Conceived by genius. Achieved by dauntless resolution and unconquerable faith."

The Wrights wanted to be remembered as individuals who had solved an age-old problem by the application of the scientific method. The record of how they achieved that end is contained in the two volumes of *The Papers of Wilbur and Orville Wright,* the details of which cannot be summarized here. The gist of their complaint against their fellow creatures is contained in a letter which Wilbur Wright wrote to Octave Chanute on January 29, 1910, and said in part:

> "As to inordinate desire for wealth, you are the only person acquainted with us who has ever made such an accusation. We believed that the physical and financial risks which we took, and the value of the service to the world, justified sufficient compensation to enable us to live modestly with enough surplus income to permit the devotion of our future time to scientific experimenting instead of business. We spent several years of valuable time trying to work out plans which would have made us independent without hampering the invention by the commercial exploitation of the patents. These efforts would have succeeded but for jealousy and envy. It was only when we found that the sale of the patents offered the only way to obtain compensation for our labors of 1900-1906 that we finally permitted the chance of making the invention free to the world to pass from our hands. You apparently concede to us no right to compensation for the solution of a problem ages old except such as is granted to persons who have no part in producing the invention. That is to say, we may compete with mountebanks for a chance to earn money in the mountebank business, but are entitled to nothing whatever for past work as inventors. If holding a different view constitutes us almost criminals, as some seem to think, we are not ashamed. We honestly think that our work of 1900-1906 has been and will be of value to the world, and that the world owes us something as inventors, regardless of whether we personally make Roman holidays for accident-loving crowds."

The balance has been redressed. The original Wright airplane occupies the place of honor in the national building devoted to telling the history of air and space and which has already been visited by millions and will be visited by many more millions as yet unborn. Nobody can fail to see and read the legend below the exhibit, the closing words of which are:

> " . . . By original scientific research the Wright Brothers discovered the principles of human flight. As inventors, builders, and flyers they further developed the aeroplane, taught man to fly, and opened the era of aviation."

The Wrights conceived of the airplane as an essentially unstable vehicle that had to be managed in the air. By analysis and argument they concluded that the essence of the flight problem lay in control and in the development of a system of control that a busy pilot could operate. Their idea of presenting the right and left wing-tips at opposite but equal angles to the air flow to create a pressure differential predated all attempts to embody it mechanically. Wilbur hit upon an immediately realizable method by twisting or deforming a bicycle tire box, an idea that was transferable by means of wires and pulleys to the wings of a biplane.

That "aileron control"—as it is now called—came early in their thinking is why Orville was still insisting to Mark Sullivan as late as 1935 that "wing-warping" was only one mechanical embodiment of an idea that was basic to the Wrights' contribution to the solution of the aviation problem. Orville was somewhat painfully aware that this was true because he had once suggested that a means of achieving this effect was a metal bar with worm gear extended from side to side through the wings of the airplane—a device much too slow and heavy to be practicable.

While the Wrights had determined at the outset that equilibrium—balance in the air—was the key to the problem, they took the up-and-down control (the front rudder, in their case, or elevator) more or less for granted and never claimed to have invented it as an independent device. It was not until October 1902 that they fully realized that their early system did not give them control about all three axes of the aircraft and that a movable rudder whose action was combined with that of the twisting wing-tips was a necessity. The remedy occurred to them both almost simultaneously, and one of the great moments of aviation history is their achievement of three-torque control—pitch, roll, and yaw. Once again, however, the thought had preceded the physical embodiment, although in the nature of things the interval was getting shorter.

What the Wrights wanted above all was the credit. This desire was neither wrong nor unnatural, but it was not a goal simply and easily attained, nor was it readily understood. Even their closest aeronautical friend, Octave Chanute, labored under a misapprehension. Hurt and doubtless angry, he wrote Wilbur that "your usually sound judgment has been warped by the desire for great wealth." If, as Wilbur said, and Orville's later life certainly proved, their desire for wealth was not inordinate, their thirst for glory may have been. Nevertheless, even in this, they were not noticeably different from others, chiefly conquerors, whose accomplishments mankind could never compensate — Alexander, Caesar, Napoleon, Lawrence, Lindbergh.

Human beings are by nature iconoclastic. They make heroes and then point at their feet of clay and pull them down from the pedestals on which they have been placed. Thus, the primacy of the Wrights in the history of aviation is not universally acknowledged to this day, and praise of them is far from automatic. It is difficult for many to concede that the first successful flight *was* the first flight.

Ferber — not always the pleasantest of men — said it all in the remark attributed to him: "To do something in the air is everything." The Wrights did everything in the air and did it first: they flew. Hedge it about with a thousand explanations, considerations, extenuations, caveats, the fact remains: they were the first men to make powered, sustained, and controlled flights.

They were not perfect, however. They never claimed to be, and I do not claim it for them. Chanute was mistaken in his remark about "the desire for great wealth," but he was not very far wrong when he told Wilbur that they underestimated their rivals. Wilbur replied with a beautiful statement which deserves repetition:

> "I am not certain that your method of estimating probabilities is a sound one. Do you not insist too strongly upon the single point of mental ability? To me it seems that a thousand other factors, each rather insignificant in itself, in the aggregate influence the event ten times more than mere mental ability or inventiveness. The world does not contain greater men than Maxim, Bell, Edison, Langley, Lilienthal, & Chanute. We are not so foolish as to base our belief (that an independent solution of the flying problem is not imminent) upon any supposed superiority to these men and to all those who will hereafter take up the problem. If the wheels of time could be turned back six years, it is not at all probable that we would do again what we have done. The one thing that impresses me as remarkable is the shortness of the time within which our work was done. It was due to peculiar combinations of circumstances which might never occur again. How do you explain the lapse of more than 50 years between Newcomen and Watt? Was the world wanting in smart men during those years? Surely not! The world was full of Watts, but a thousand and one trifles kept them from undertaking and completing the task. I do not doubt that the world today contains hundreds of men as able as Napoleon but, if a war should break out, I would consider it safe to bet a thousand to one that a second Napoleon would not appear. We look upon the present question in an entirely impersonal way. It is not chiefly a question of relative ability, but of mathematical probabilities. The fact that lightning strikes once in some particular spot is no evidence that it will strike there again soon. And yet the fact that it may do so is sufficient to enforce prudence."

Wilbur's statement was right to the extent that it ruled out inevitability. It was wrong in assuming — rather blindly — that the secrets, if secrets there were, were not out. Had not Chanute revealed them in Paris talks in 1903, later published with pictures? True, the pictures were not a blueprint, but they were very informative. It is also a fact that no European flew for more than a full minute until November 1907 and for more than two minutes until March 1908, but Europeans were on their way, and a practical flyer was not, as Wilbur argued in the fall of 1906, five or ten years away. The Wrights themselves believed that a patent was a disclosure, and their first patent was granted on May 22, 1906. They had been exceedingly careful to see that, broad and all-encompassing though it was, it disclosed as little as possible of the constructions and combinations of their airplane, but the margin of security was less than Wilbur calculated. If the French had believed that the Wrights were flyers, and not liars, the margin would have been even less, and the Wrights' priority even harder to believe. Nothing can detract from Wilbur's triumph in France in August and Orville's at Fort Myer in September 1908, even though Orville's trials were cut short by the crash that killed Selfridge and injured Orville. They and their airplane were the toast of two continents. The net effect, however, was to spur others along.

Orville's accident led the Wrights to make what in my opinion was another error of judgment, which was the result of sentimentality and perhaps even of arrogance. By all odds, Wilbur should have flown the Channel and not have left the honor to Blériot who, by a fluke, beat out Latham. *The Daily Mail* prize of £1000 was established by Lord Northcliffe specifically for Wilbur to win. Before anyone else, Northcliffe realized the strategic significance of the airplane. He said: "The news is not that Wilbur Wright has flown, but that England is no longer an island." To dramatize this truth, Northcliffe not only set up the *Daily Mail* prize but went so far as to offer Wilbur privately a handsome bonus if he would fly the Channel first. The newspaper magnate's interest was far more to demonstrate the truth of his premise than to promote a contest between developing airplanes.

It was not to be, however. Orville, recuperating from his Fort Myer accident, asked Wilbur not to attempt the flight until they could be together, one brother flying, the other checking things on the ground. The request should have been overruled as the superstition it was, but a *crise de confiance* had momentarily seized Orville, and Wilbur—who, be it noted, was present at Fort Myer for the continuation of the U. S. Army acceptance trials—agreed not to make the Channel flight alone. The timetable of aviation, favoring the Wrights, was irretrievably overturned. It is far from my purpose to cast any shadows on Blériot. He made a glorious flight in a doubtful airplane and deserved every farthing he won and the fame.

The Wrights have been correctly credited with developing the airplane. Their Huffman Prairie machine of 1905 and their passenger-carrying Kitty Hawk machine of 1908 were vast improvements over the original and some- what primitive machine of 1903. Indeed, the advance was so great that without the practical machines that followed so rapidly the flights of 1903 would have seemed scarcely credible.

It is true that the Wrights made many improvements in the airplane in later years, although—rather inexplicably—some things that lay entirely in their power to accomplish were put off until the credit had passed to others. Any tally of developments left incomplete, untried, or postponed would have to include the perfection of pontoons and the development of the hydro-air-plane, landing on and taking off from a ship, the substitution of tractor for pusher propulsion, the abandonment of the clever but cumbersome bicycle-chain drive, the adoption of wheels in place of the skids originally necessi-tated by the sands of Kitty Hawk, and the use of a closed-in cockpit and fuselage with the advantage that the latter offered in side surface. While it is easy to criticize, the explanation seems to lie with their overriding concern for what they had already achieved.

Let us be content with the Wrights as they were. We are always asking of genius more than genius is ready and willing to perform. It is a privilege that is not necessarily ours. The immortality of the Wrights is assured. They designed, built, and flew the first airplane. They discovered and established on a scientific basis the principles of human flight. They taught themselves and the rest of mankind to fly. They developed the airplane to a point of high practical success and demonstrated its capabilities to the world.

In connection with the celebration of the fiftieth anniversary of the first flight, I wrote, in *The Papers of Wilbur and Orville Wright*, in the introduc-tion:

> "The navigation by man of the ocean of air in which the globe is immersed has been possible for so short a time that the whole history of it is comprehended by the memory of living men. But already it is clear that the realization of this immemorial human dream has brought with it changes in the relationship of individuals, of peoples, of states, and even—it may soon not be farfetched to say—of worlds, so fundamental that its influence must be felt, with growing effect, over many more generations. The instrument of this revolution is the aeroplane. Its creation by Wilbur and Orville Wright and its progress in their hands during its emergent years are the subject of this work."

When he walked on the moon in July 1969, closely followed by Edwin "Buzz" Aldrin while Michael Collins orbited in the lonely Command Module, Neil Armstrong said: "That's one small step for a man . . . one giant leap for man-kind." About to take their first step, Wilbur and Orville Wright meant much the same thing when they telegraphed after their trial of December 14, 1903: "Success assured. Keep quiet."

BIBLIOGRAPHY

Bonnalie, Allan F. "They Still Look to the Wrights," *Pegasus*, Dec. 1953, vol. 23, pp. 5-7, illus.

Cortwright, Edgar M. (ed.) *Apollo Expeditions to the Moon*. NASA SP-350. Washington, D. C. 1975, pp. 203-224.

Langewiesche, Wolfgang. "What the Wrights Really Invented," *Harper's Magazine*, June 1950, vol. 200, pp. 102-105.

Gibbs-Smith, Charles H. *The Aeroplane: an Historical Survey of Its Origins and Development.* London, 1960.

See especially pp. 35-44, pp. 62-64, and pp. 224-234 for material on the Wrights.

McFarland, Marvin W. "A Look at Aviation Fifty-Three Years After," *U.S. Air Services,* Dec. 1956, vol. 41, pp. 5-6.

McFarland, Marvin W. "When the Airplane Was a Military Secret: A Study of National Attitudes Before 1914," *U.S. Air Services,* Sept. 1954, vol. 39, pp. 11, 14, 16; Oct. 1954, vol. 39, pp 18, 20-22.

Wright, Orville. *How We Invented the Aeroplane.* Edited and with Commentary by Fred C. Kelly. Drawings by James MacDonald. New York: 1953.

Wright, Wilbur, and Wright, Orville. *The Papers of Wilbur and Orville Wright, Including the Chanute-Wright Letters and Other Papers of Octave Chanute.* Marvin W. McFarland, editor. New York, 1953. 2 v.

McFarland, Marvin W. "The Wright Brothers' Aeroplane," *The Century Magazine,* Sept. 1908, vol. 76, pp. 641-650, illus.

MARVIN WILKS MCFARLAND, born in Philadelphia, Pa., was educated at Girard College, took his B.A. degree at Franklin and Marshall College in 1940, and did graduate work at McGill University, Montreal, Canada, and at Georgetown University, Washington, D.C. He served as research assistant to the Librarian, Girard College, 1940-1941, and as an assistant in the Manuscripts Department of the Historical Society of Pennsylvania until he was called into the service in 1942.

He rose from private to captain, U.S. Army Air Forces and U.S. Air Force, in which organizations he served until September 1948. In that period, he was chief archivist, U.S. Strategic Air Forces in Europe; a member of the U.S. shuttle-bombing group in the U.S.S.R.; assistant historian, USSTAF, London, England; and finally staff assistant to General Carl Spaatz, the first Chief of Staff, U.S. Air Force. McFarland joined the staff of the Library of Congress in October 1948, filling the Guggenheim Chair of Aeronautics for a period of ten years until becoming Assistant Chief, Science and Technology Division, in 1963. He has been Chief of that Division, including the National Referral Center, since 1966.

In 1953, he edited *The Papers of Wilbur and Orville Wright;* was contributing editor, *U.S. Air Services* magazine, 1956; consultant and contributed two chapters to *The American Heritage History of Flight,* 1962; consultant for the American Heritage Junior Library publication series, *The Air War Against Hitler's Germany,* 1964; and has written numerous articles for aviation, aerospace, and library journals. He has been active in many aviation and library organizations and has won a number of prizes and awards. Another volume comprising the Wrights' letters to each other, *Dear Wilbur, Dear Orville,* is scheduled for publication in 1979.

The Wright Brothers: Their Influence

CHARLES H. GIBBS-SMITH

An abiding and vital problem with almost any historian is the influence that his subject exerts on his contemporaries or on those that follow him. There is no more distressing case than a man or woman of great talent who is forced to work in a vacuum, or in such circumstances that their work influences nothing or nobody.

There are, furthermore, certain historic people who are deliberately and posthumously forced into a position where their opponents — in fact their enemies, more often than not — seek to show that despite the admitted nature and caliber of their work, they toiled to no practical avail. Inventors are particularly prone to this sort of contrived situation, which may be subtly suggested or openly stated. The Wright brothers have been subjected both to the accusation that they were not the first to fly, and the more insidious accusation that if by chance they are proved to have been the first, then it made no difference in history because they worked in secret, and that others were ignorant of their work and followed their own paths to success and fame independently of anything the Wrights might have accomplished. This supposition was well put some years ago by an English correspondent in *Flight* magazine,[1] who wrote:

> "These facts emerge inexorably as a result of a dispassionate approach to the subject and are as follows:
> (a) the aeroplane as we know it today is wholly European (and primarily French) both in concept and development;
> (b) That if the Wright brothers had never lived, the aeroplane would still have been conceived in Europe by the same people at the same times and would have proceeded through the same stages of development that in fact, it did.
> Any attempt to deny the foregoing is not only a distortion of history, but inflicts a grave injustice on the true creators of the modern

1. *Flight International*, August 13, 1966.

aeroplane—people like the Voisin brothers, Blériot, Levavasseur, Breguet, Goupy, A. V. Roe, and a host of others."

Those with a personal axe to grind have made an even more dramatic bid to push the Wrights out of the picture. Here is pioneer Gabriel Voisin,[2] for example, who claimed to have invented the aeroplane for the glory of both himself and of France (his italics):

"America, with unbelievable insolence, claims to have been the birthplace of aviation. It is inconceivable that France should bow before so naive a claim. Aviation was born in France, and not one of our great men, true pioneers of the air, borrowed anything at all from the men of Dayton. The Super-Fortresses, the Constellations and the jet-driven Boeings, owe their origins to Ader's *Avion* of 1897 and to that of Blériot in 1909, while the most up-to-date *Lightning* leaves in its slipstream remembrances of the old Voisin of 1908 . . . . We never had at any time during our work communications relating to their [the Wrights'] arrangements, and when my brother finally succeeded, on 30 March 1907, at Bagatelle, in making the first French powered flight recorded on film, the totality of French constructors *had no knowledge of the Wrights or of their work.* In a word, the existence of the two Americans never influenced our researchers in any way. . . . No technician of real standing can admit that the Wrights inspired anything at all, and that for two reasons. The first is important: the Wrights kept their secret so well that it remained impenetrable from 1903 to 8 August 1908, a date by which French aviation was definitely under way. The second reason also has its significance: *the Wright aircraft had no future.* When the Wrights came to France, financed by influential people, and with resources we could never have hoped for, praised to the skies by a (largely paid) press, it taught us nothing. . . . At the moment when his boat left the shores of France—which had welcomed him with an almost unbelievable enthusiasm—Wilbur Wright, had he been able to peer through the Channel fog, would have distinguished the shadow of the Blériot XII [XI], the aircraft which was to be carried to England on the wings of victory. Then he might have realized the uselessness of his efforts, the poverty of his devices, and the futility of his secrets."

En passant, it is amusing to note that Blériot relied on a direct copy of the Wrights' wing-warping for the most important element in his flight-control system! And the idea of anyone owing anything to Ader is so risible as to be grotesque.

If one has patience enough to study the documents and photographs of those all-important years in Europe, 1902 to 1908, one finds that the French pioneers were aware of everything the Wrights achieved, by way of a constant stream of information and photographs from Octave Chanute, the Wrights

---

2. G. Voisin, *Men, Women and 10,000 Kites* (London, 1963), p. 238.

themselves, their own French publications — particularly *L'Aérophile* — and other informants from America.[3]

It will be recalled that the Wrights made their first machine, a wing-warping kite, in 1899; then their three gliders (1900-02) culminated in the modified No. 3 glider (1902) which incorporated full three-axis control, *i.e.* pitch, yaw and roll. Then came the first three powered *Flyers*, as they were called, from 1903 to 1905. The Wright *Flyer III* of 1905 was the world's first practical aeroplane. It could fly for more than half an hour at a time, and could bank, turn, circle and do figures of eight, all with the greatest of ease and grace. Next, after an interval, they flew in public for the first time in 1908. In addition, Wilbur Wright gave two public lectures at Chicago in 1901 and 1903, both of which were circulated widely in America and Europe.

The Continental influence of the Wrights began in 1902 when European aviation was virtually at a standstill, Lilienthal having been killed 1896 and Pilcher in 1899, the main line of development in Europe was almost at a standstill, with the exception of the French artillery Captain Ferdinand Ferber. He was just keeping the ball rolling, so to speak, with a feeble imitation of a Lilienthal glider in 1901. Charles Dollfus describes him as "the great French percursor of practical aviation: he was the first in our country to build, and test methodically, full-size gliders." In 1902 Ferber made contact with Chanute: was told by him about the Wrights; and immediately adopted the Wright glider configuration. In his own book *L'Aviation* (1909) he headed one of his chapters "Ferber in Pursuit of the Wrights, from 1902 to 1906," and he built what he admitted were copies of the Wright gliders. In April of 1903 Chanute both lectured on the Wrights in Paris and published two articles in France detailing, as far as he could, the Wright type of glider. This gave a further powerful boost to the fashion for building Wright-type gliders. Ferber himself, in 1903, started a correspondence with the Wrights, which led to them keeping him *au courant* with what they were doing right through 1905: Ferber then saw that his French contemporaries were thus informed of the Wrights' growing successes.

In 1903, in addition to Ferber, we find the well-known French pioneer Ernest Archdeacon first describing the Wright glider configuration, "their [the Wrights'] last machine appears actually to be the model of its kind. I will therefore describe only this machine. . ." Then he used his powerful influence to try and persuade his confréres to get going, sometimes writing angrily, as when he says in 1903 (his italics):

> "France, this great homeland of inventors, assuredly does not hold the lead *in the special science of* AVIATION, even when the majority of good minds are today convinced that this alone is the true way. Will the homeland of Montgolfier have the shame of allowing this ultimate discovery of aerial science — which is certainly imminent, and which will constitute the greatest scientific revolution that has been since the

3. All further references and quoted sections can be found in the author's *The Rebirth of European Aviation: 1902-1908* (London, 1974).

beginning of the world — to be realised abroad? You scholars, to your compasses! You, the maecenases; and you, too, Gentlemen of the Government; put your hands in your pockets — or else we are beaten!"

And the Count de La Vaulx writes, also in 1903, "Archdeacon decided to shake our aviators out of their torpor, and put a stop to the indifference of French opinion concerning flying-machines." The doyen of French aviation historians, Charles Dollfus, wrote of Chanute's Paris lecture:

"This communication had a decisive importance: it orientated French aviation towards an attempt at imitating the Wright gliders."

At the end of 1903 the news of the Wrights' powered flights on December 17 of that year reached France, and Ferber writes (his italics):

"Although the results were less remarkable than was announced at first, the date December 17th 1903 nonetheless marks the day when a *piloted* flying machine *has really flown*, and the honour of this memorable experiment falls to the name of Wright."

In the year 1904, Ferber was again to comment:

"Archdeacon is very active, and hence I believe that not fewer than 6 apparatuses of the 1902 Wright type are now being built in France. I believe we will see a great movement."

Archdeacon's own machine (his first glider) was, in his own words, "a machine which is, apart from subsequent modifications, exactly copied from that of the Wright brothers."

Then Victor Tatin, one of the most respected of the early French pioneers, made a speech to the *Aéro-Club de France*, which was quoted as including the following:

"In closing, M. Tatin protested against the tendency we seem to have in France of slavishly copying the gliding machines of the Americans. . . . And then, where do such copies lead us? Does this not seem like a confession of our incapacity to make anything original ourselves?"

Also in 1903, Tatin wrote a more desperate appeal:

"Must we one day read in history that aviation, born in France, only became successful thanks to the Americans; and that the French only obtained results by slavishly copying them? For us, that would indeed be glorious! Have we not already seen enough French inventions completed by foreigners, . . . "

"To obtain anything from inventors in France," he continued, "it is necessary to stimulate rivalry . . . "

Meanwhile, the Wrights kept Ferber current with their latest achievements; and even the United Kingdom, which was more or less moribund from the flying point of view, learned from their own sources what the Wrights were doing, and how successful they were.

The year 1905 saw a continuing series of abject failures on the Continent. Another famous name in France, Robert Esnault-Pelterie, was to go on record:

"We constructed an aeroplane scrupulously following the directions of the Wright brothers, directions and diagrams which, moreover, were published in *L'Aérophile*. Our machine was exactly like that of the American experimenters, as much as to the general dimensions as to the curvature of the ribs and the disposition of the controls. Only some questions of construction and detail were different."

Meanwhile, Ferber was bravely fitting a small and ineffectual engine to one of his gliders: but he was pessimistic:

"It is thus that, taking solely to the Wright type in 1902, I am two years behind him [*i.e.* Wilbur Wright] and I have not yet been able to catch up, whilst I retain a similar advance over my pupils. The reason for this is that to achieve practicality is always a long, difficult, and costly business."

The French press formed another link between the Wrights and France. We find the correspondent of *L'Auto*, Robert Coquelle, writing: "I have interviewed the witnesses, and it is impossible to doubt the success of their experiments."

It was also in 1905 that a pirated drawing of the Wrights' powered *Flyer III* was published in France, and the redoubtable Ferber commented:

"This drawing had great importance; it showed us the last details of which we were ignorant; and it was this drawing which caused the first aeroplanes of Delagrange and Farman — February and June of 1907 — to have a forward cellular rudder [elevator]."

Most of the French gliders of the period copied the configuration of biplane structure and forward monoplane elevator of the Wright gliders. Now we see the origins, to be adopted in France in 1907, of the biplane elevator out front, on the early Voisin biplanes, deriving from the biplane elevators of the powered Wright Flyers.

The year 1906 saw the first groping steps towards powered flying in Europe, and the Wrights' influence, having conditioned the first basic configurations on the Continent, continued as an infuriating spectre which was always hovering behind the French, and looking over their shoulders to torment them. News of the triumphant 1905 season of the Wrights was gathering thick and fast in Europe. Some of the French buried their heads in the sand, but the wisest of them knew better. Tatin, more respected than any other pioneer, had this to say:

"The glory of having obtained the first results is therefore forever lost to France, which was nevertheless the cradle of aviation, and was for such a long time at the head of other nations in the matter of research. Unfortunately, for some years, in spite of all that could be stimulating from the news reaching us of the partial success and the well-founded hopes of the Americans, we have remained in a regrettable state of expectancy, when we had here in France all that was necessary to resolve—better and more rapidly—the problem of which the solution abroad has today aroused us; but aroused us a little too late, alas!"

To make matters worse, the press even announced that Santos-Dumont, who made the first tentative European flights at the end of this year 1906, had been driven to abandon airships and take up aviation following the revelations of what the Wrights were doing. Archdeacon wrote a rousing manifesto to urge his compatriots to do better, and build successful aeroplanes; and the President of the *Aéro-Club de France* praised this document as a means "to shake us out of our inexcusable torpor."

By 1907 a few French aeroplanes were making small hops, but no European pilot could stay in the air for a whole minute until late in this year. Ferber, in a burst of excitement after meeting Wilbur Wright, wrote:

"Just think that without this man I would be nothing, for I should not have dared, in 1902, to trust myself on a flimsy fabric if I had not known from his accounts and his photographs that it would carry me! Think that without him, my experiments would not have taken place, and I should not have had Voisin as a pupil. Capitalists like Archdeacon and Deutsch de la Meurthe would not in 1904 have established the prizes you know of. The press would not have spread the good seed on all sides. Your magazine [L'Aérophile] would not have quadrupled its circulation, and other special journals would not have been born!"

But the Europeans, even in their short-hop flights in 1907 and 1908, still had no clear conception of flight control, and the final and decisive influence of the Wrights on Europe came with Wilbur's outstanding flights in France from August 1908 through 1909. This influence was simply the demonstration of full three-axis flight control. As the eminent Frenchman Count de La Vaulx put it, speaking of Wilbur's aeroplane, "this machine, which had just revolutionized the aviator's world."

A great chorus of ovation from the French greeted Wilbur's flying, and the accounts coming out of France were almost delirious in their surprise, praise, and adulation. No adjective was too extreme, no comment more ecstatic, than those that came from the mouths of the continental pioneers. To sum it up, here is Charles Dollfus:

"Wilbur Wright came to France, and gave at the Hunaudières racecourse, and then at the Camp d'Auvours—in the neighborhood of Le Mans—a series of flights which were sensational, and constitute a decisive epoch of history. The first flight took place on August 8th 1908. Numerous flights followed, revolutionising aviation by the excellence of the pilotage, the manageableness, and the versatility of the machine."

CHARLES HARVARD GIBBS-SMITH is currently the first Lindbergh Professor of Aerospace History at the National Air and Space Museum. He came to the Smithsonian from London, where he is a Research Fellow at the Science Museum. He started writing official works on aviation history for the Science Museum in 1960, and has now written twenty publications on the subject, twelve of them for the Museum. Mr. Gibbs-Smith is an Honorary Companion of the British Royal Aeronautical Society, and was a research fellow and master of arts of Harvard University. He is also an adjunct fellow of the Woodrow Wilson International Center for Scholars at the Smithsonian Institution. Among works on other subjects, he has published three novels.

Popular Attitudes Towards Aviation, 1900-1925

The Airplane, The Wrights, and The American Public

ROGER E. BILSTEIN

In 1908, a curious 14 year-old named Charles Fayette Taylor found an article written by Orville and Wilbur Wright in *Century Magazine.* It was the brothers' first account of their own development of the airplane to be published in a popular periodical. Vastly taken by this story, young Charles showed it to his father. Despite the accompanying photos, the elder Taylor refused to accept the notion that human flight was a reality.[1] Undaunted, young Charles persisted in aviation, becoming a prominent aero engineer and professor at the Massachusetts Institute of Technology. One assumes that his doubting parent was eventually convinced that the Wrights had actually achieved what they claimed in 1908.

But the son's reaction and his father's skepticism typified the ambivalence toward airplanes that characterized the American public during the pre-World War I years. For all the evidence that accumulated in other published reports before 1908 and after, most Americans had to see it to believe it. The airplane, the Wrights, and the American public eventually came to terms in the course of a turbulent and flamboyant era of aviation development.

As the world calendar passed from 1899 into the twentieth century, many informed individuals regarded the prospects of manned aircraft with reasonable confidence. Samuel Brooks Adams savored the feast of essays celebrating the past and future sent him by his old friend from the Smithsonian, Samuel Pierpont Langley, including the reports and photographs of Langley's model "aerodromes" in flight.[2] These early experiments, along with the glider flights of Lilienthal and others, were know to Adams and scores of Americans who read Smithsonian publications and journals like the *Scientific American.* Thousands of Americans had witnessed balloon flights. Across the country in the late nineteenth century, many newspapers commented fa-

1. Charles Fayette Taylor, "Aircraft Propulsion: a Review of Aircraft Powerplants," Smithsonian Institution, *Annual Report* (1962), p. 251. The Wright brothers' article, entitled "Wright Brothers Aeroplane," appeared in *Century Magazine,* LXXVI (September, 1908), pp. 641-50.

2. Ernest Samuel, *Henry Adams: The Major Phase* (Cambridge, Massachusetts, 1964), pp. 242-43.

vorably on the prospects of powered flight, and numbers of enthusiasts were attempting to develop a feasible airplane.[3] Still, a considerable segment of the American public harbored strong doubts about the notion of human flight in a winged aircraft powered by an engine. Mark Sullivan, one of the eminent journalists of the day, vividly recalled an informal dinner in 1901 with Langley and Alexander Graham Bell at Bell's home in Nova Scotia. Bell strongly believed in airplanes, as opposed to balloons, and remarked to Langley that piloted airplanes would someday be able to fly off with cargos as heavy as a thousand bricks. Sullivan's reaction was to remind himself that Bell had invented the telephone, and that feat alone entitled him to considerable latitude in predicting the future. Also, Bell was an old man—he had a right to ruminate any way he pleased. But to himself, Sullivan was thinking, "he is talking plain nonsense."[4]

Sullivan was not alone. During 1901, leading popular periodicals like *McClure's Magazine* and the *North American Review* still published articles that discussed flying machines in the most condescending terms. One contribution in *McClure's* was written by Simon Newcomb, an internationally known astronomer and mathematician at Johns Hopkins. "Man's desire to fly like a bird is inborn in our race," he wrote, "and we can no more be expected to abandon the idea than the ancient mathematician could have been expected to give up the problem of squaring the circle."[5] Other publications were just as negative on the subject, using the flying machine as a vehicle for stock humor in the same genre as "mother-in-law" jokes, and the inane yarns that began with the tip-off phrase, "there were two Irishmen." People who attempted to build flying machines fell into the same category as notorious cranks trying to make perpetual motion machines, tunnel through the world to China, or perpetuate similar fantasies. As one humorist jibed in the magazine *Puck* (in 1904, nearly a year after the Wright's success), hopeful airplane inventors would get into the air as soon as the law of gravity could be repealed.[6] It was in this controversial atmosphere that Langley attempted to fly his full-size airplane, the Aerodrome.

The elderly Langley turned over controls of the Aerodrome to his co-worker, Charles Manly, who had developed the plane's remarkable gasoline engine. Late in the autumn of 1903, the Aerodrome failed in two attempts to launch into flight by means of a catapult built atop a houseboat anchored in the Potomac, and Manly received two highly publicized duckings in the river. The Washington *Post*, which had derisively dubbed Langley's flying machine the

3. Tom D. Crouch, "To Ride the Fractious Horse: The American Aeronautical Community and the Problem of Heavier-Than-Air Flight, 1875-1905," Ph.D. dissertation, The Ohio State University (1976). See, especially, Chapter 10.

4. Mark Sullivan, *Our Times: The United States, 1900-1925* (New York, 1927) vol. II, p. 558, note 1.

5. Simon Newcomb, "Is the Airship Coming," *McClure's Magazine*, XVII (September, 1901), p. 434.

6. Sullivan, *Our Times*, II, pp. 556-57.

"Buzzard," gleefully reported Langley's lack of success, and other published accounts jeered at the "Smithsonian staff, the stuffers of birds and rabbits...." Langley's soggy fiasco on the Potomac elicited an outpouring of smug criticism from newspapers like the Chicago *Tribune,* who had known all along that God intended mortal men to remain grounded until the roll was called in Heaven. The Boston *Herald* recommended that Langley re-direct his efforts towards submarine development, since his handiwork seemed to have more affinity for water than air. The diatribe against the Aerodrome poured in from high and low, including a devastating comment from the mordant Ambrose Bierce: "I don't know how much larger Professor Langley's machine is than his flying model was — about large enough, I think, to require an atmosphere a little denser than the intelligence of one scientist and not quite so dense as that of two."[7]

In short, Langley's unhappy efforts to achieve airplane flight hardened the convictions of most Americans that the notion was totally impractical. If Langley, with his academic training, scientific background, and prestigious backing, could not do it, then who could? Crazy scientists who wanted to toy with the unremitting law of gravity had been given their come-uppance. Common sense would show up a college degree and other fancy credentials any day of the week.[8]

Langley's second failure occurred on December 8, 1903. Nine days later, at Kill Devil Hill, near Kitty Hawk, North Carolina, the Wright brothers flew into history.

For the next five years, the Wright's Promethean achievement remained virtually unknown, and several available accounts that surfaced were badly garbled. The Wrights themselves had personally issued a statement to the Associated Press in January, 1904, attempting to clarify some of the gross misinformation about their plane and the Kitty Hawk flight, but the gesture had little effect. Accurate stories by acquaintances and first-hand observors were, surprisingly, ignored. In remarks to a meeting of the American Association for the Advancement of Science early that year, Octave Chanute reported the Wrights' success at Kitty Hawk, and used this address as a basis for an article appearing in the March, 1904, issue of *Popular Science Monthly.* In September, Amos I. Root, publisher of a well known apiary journal in Medina, Ohio, came to Dayton out of curiosity, saw the Wrights fly (a performance that included the first complete circle flown by an airplane), and recorded his impressions. Thus, history's first published, eye-witness account of a flight appeared in 1905 — and was presented in a periodical with a most unlikely title: *Gleanings in Bee Culture.*[9]

7. For this sampling of news accounts, see, Harold U. Faulkner, *The Quest for Social Justice, 1898-1914* (New York, 1931), pp. 137-38; and Sullivan, *Our Times,* II, pp. 562-67, which includes the quote from Bierce.

8. Sullivan, *Ibid.*

9. Fred C. Kelly, *The Wright Brothers* (New York, 1943), pp. 105-11, 117-19. The full text of Amos Root's charming and didactic account is reprinted in C. H. Gibbs-Smith, *The Aeroplane: An Historical Survey of Its Origins and Development* (London, 1960), pp. 234-39.

Continuing skepticism and the Langley debacle apparently discouraged nearly everyone from seriously considering persistent rumors emanating from Kitty Hawk or Huffman Prairie, the field near Dayton where the two brothers regularly flew within sight of a well-travelled trolley line. Irregular news stories during the next few years were often highly inaccurate, and were either spurned by editors or cautiously reported with elaborate disclaimers. Years later, Orville commented on this puzzling reluctance of the American public to believe in airplanes: "I think it was mainly due to the fact that human flight was generally looked upon as an impossibility, and that scarcely anyone believed in it until he actually saw it with his own eyes." Although the Wrights invited a few reporters to Huffman Prairie on at least two occasions, mechanical problems and poor weather prohibited flights, and the newsmen left with their skepticism vindicated. Even the Dayton *Daily News* remained blasé. In any case, the Wrights themselves remained reticent about too much publicity until they felt their patent rights were secure and they had perfected certain working details.[10]

Still, there was a small but influential number of Americans and some journalists who believed that the Wrights had flown. By late 1906, the *Scientific American* had editorially acknowledged the Wrights' success, and the brothers were beginning to assess the potential uses of their airplane. As Wilbur confided to Chanute late in 1904, "it is a question whether we are not ready to begin considering what we will do with our baby now that we have it."[11]

With innate thoroughness, the Wrights projected a possible sequence of acceptance: planes would first be useful for military reconnaissance, and then for exploration, speedy transportation of passengers and freight, including mail, and finally for sport. It appears that the Wrights hoped that airplanes might actually prevent wars by representing an awesome military deterrent. Given the state of the art in 1904, however, aerial surveillance represented the earliest military potential, although commercial applications seemed promising. "It is therefore our intention to furnish machines for military use first, before entering the commercial field," Orville announced, "but we reserve the right to exploit our invention in any manner we think proper." As the Wrights expected, military officials finally made the first move towards adopting the airplane. After considerable delay and some uneasiness, as the Wrights negotiated with Great Britain, France, and Ger-

10. Orville Wright to Mark Sullivan in 1925, quoted in Sullivan, *Our Times*, II, p. 599, note 1; Kelly, *Wright Brothers*, pp. 135-46; Henry Ladd Smith, *Airways: The Story of Commercial Aviation in the United States* (New York, 1942), pp. 21-22; C. H. Gibbs-Smith, *Aviation: An Historical Survey from Its Origins to the End of World War II* (London, 1970), p. 102.

11. Kelly, *Wright Brothers*, pp. 143-46; Fred C. Kelly, ed., *Miracle at Kitty Hawk: The Letters of Wilbur and Orville Wright* (New York, 1951), p. 133.

12. Roger E. Bilstein, "Putting Aircraft to Work: The First Air Freight," *Ohio History*, LXXVI (Autumn, 1967), p. 249; Kelly, *Wright Brothers*, p. 204, note 1; Wright brothers to War Department (June 15, 1907) in Kelly, *Kitty Hawk*, p. 216.

many, the United States War Department concluded a contract for $25,000 in February 1908, and became the owners of one flying machine following successful flight demonstrations in the summer of 1909.[12]

The years 1908-1909 brought wide publicity and belated acclaim. Orville's tests for the War Department at Ft. Meyer, Virginia, and Wilbur's flights in Europe before enthralled crowds, including kings of Spain and England, became convincing front-page news, while the flights of other pioneers like Glenn Curtiss stirred additional interest in aviation. With increasing acceptance, the time had come to look forward to practical use. "I firmly believe in the future of the aeroplane for commerce, to carry mail, to carry passengers, perhaps express," Orville wrote. "I cannot but believe that we stand at the beginning of a new era, the Age of Flight, and that the beginnings of today will be mightily overshadowed by the complete successes of tomorrow."[13]

But the age of flight was immature. The general public, reluctantly becoming convinced that flight was an actuality, considered it too much of a novelty to be taken seriously. When a Texas Congressman introduced a bill to investigate airmail operations in 1910, the New York *Telegraph* found the idea ludicrous. "Love letters will be carried in a rose-pink aeroplane," the paper scoffed, "Steered with Cupid's wings and operated by perfumed gasoline." Such public skepticism stemmed from the flamboyant character of aviation at the time. As a sensational mechanical contraption, "aeroplanes" received their first wide public exposure as star attractions in aerial exhibitions that featured various flying stunts. The attendant ballyhoo and publicity propagated the notion that airplanes were hazardous and their pilots were daredevils and fools. People were willing to pay to observe the marvel of flight and to be on hand for the deliciously chilling prospect of an airplane smashup. Professional impresarios like Barnum and Bailey knew a box office attraction when they saw one. As early as 1907, they had contacted the Wright brothers about the possibilities of flying exhibitions, a natural act for "The Greatest Show on Earth." Although the Wrights were more inclined to deal with the United States Army than the circus, military purchases were not numerous and the civilian market was necessarily limited. At $5,000 to $7,500 per plane, a flying machine remained a rich man's gadget. The negligible payload continued to discourage commercial operations, which in any case would have foundered on the lack of permanent landing fields, hangars, and maintenance facilities. The scarcity of revenue prompted the Wright brothers and Glenn Curtiss to organize their own exhibition companies and retain some of the daring fraternity of "birdmen" to fly in them.[14]

For their air show manager, the Wrights hired Roy Knabenshue, an experienced promoter in the aerial show business of ballooning, and began to train additional pilots. During 1910, Orville Wright organized flying schools at

13. Orville Wright, "Future of the Aeroplane," *Country Life*, LV (January, 1909), pp. 252-53.
14. Bilstein, "Putting Aircraft to Work," p. 250; New York *Telegraph* (June 19, 1910).

Montgomery, Alabama (for training in the winter months) and at Huffman Prairie. Early fliers trained at these locations included Walter Brookins, Arch Hoxsey, Ralph Johnstone, Phil O. Parmalee, Frank T. Coffyn, and others, including future military fliers like General Henry H. "Hap" Arnold. There was nothing glamorous about these early flight schools. The training field at Huffman Prairie was still little more than a cow pasture. The field was a bit marshy, and more than one errant trainee had to have his plane hauled out of the mud while trying to get airborne. A wooden shed at one end of the field served as a hangar, while at the other end stood a large thorn tree, a menacing sentinal. Under Knabenshue's direction, the Wright Exhibition Company and its newly minted pilots hit the road in 1910, playing at carnivals, circuses, county fairs, and anything else that promised a crowd and reasonable gate receipts. For the privilege of billing their flying show at such gatherings, the Wrights charged $5,000 for each plane used. Fliers got a base pay of $20.00 per week, plus $50.00 per day when they flew. At these prices, pilots like Frank Coffyn earned $6,000 to $7,000 per season, and the Wright Exhibition Company grossed about $1 million per year. Aviation had become a business.[15]

Additional aerial exhibition teams, like the one organized by Glenn Curtiss, soon made their appearance, and specially organized flying meets became major spectator events, attracting thousands of people in a single day. Most of the crowd came to be convinced. As Beckwith Havens, a Curtiss pilot recalled, "They thought you were a fake, you see. There wasn't anybody there who believed [an airplane] would really fly. In fact, they'd give odds. But when you flew, oh my, they'd carry you off the field. . . ." During 1910, the sky seemed to blossom with airmen and airplanes, not only at county fairs, but at major flying meets across the country. One of the most publicized affairs was the worldwide meet at Belmont Park, Long Island, during 1910. Participants included top fliers from Great Britain, France, and the United States. Perhaps the salient feature of the meet was the fact that it became a society sporting event, and social elite in attendance included Harold McCormick of Chicago and Cornelius Vanderbilt, who went up for a spin with Orville Wright. The same year, ex-President Theodore Roosevelt ventured aloft as a passenger in a Wright plane piloted by Arch Hoxsey, who had to caution Roosevelt against waving too exuberantly at the crowd below. The prominent names associated with aerial events did much to increase the prestige and acceptance of aviation. After a meet at Los Angeles attracted over 30,000

15. Kelly, *Wright Brothers*, pp. 273-75 Henry H. Arnold, *Global Mission* (New York, 1941), p. 16; Grover Loening, *Takeoff Into Greatness* (New York, 1968), p. 44; interviews of Thomas Milling and Frank Coffyn, housed in *The Oral History Collection of Columbia University*, New York City, Cited hereafter as OHC.

16. Interviews of Thomas Milling and Bechwith Havens, OHC; editors of *Year: Flight, A Pictorial History of Aviation* (Los Angeles, 1953), p. 54; Smith, *Airways*, p. 29; Glenn H. Curtiss and Augustus Post, *The Curtiss Aviation Book* (New York, 1912), pp. 166-67.

people on a Sunday afternoon in 1911, Glenn Curtiss was moved to say, "I am convinced . . . that aviation is a standard and lasting thing."[16]

Increasing numbers of passengers took to the air, and these early recollections are vivid vignettes of a unique new experience. As one anonymous writer remembered his first air trip:

> The worst part of such a journey for the novice is the waiting until everything is ready for the start. The sensation of anticipation is not unlike the feeling that one has when one is waiting for a wounded bear to break cover from the corner into which he is driven. But once the propellor starts to whirl behind you all other thoughts beyond rapid exhilaration of motion vanish.

The author even relaxed the deathhold he had taken on the struts, and after the four-minute spin, it seemed ". . . the most delightful ride that I had ever experienced. The only recollection that I have that will describe the general sensation is that of exquisite motion." While talking to an interviewer one day in 1913, Ida Tarbell spoke of her faith in aviation, though admitting she had never flown. Hearing of the interview, the editor of *Flying* magazine, Henry Woodhouse, arranged for a flight in a hydroplane. Miss Tarbell, a worldly wise, muckraking journalist, was overwhelmed. The pilot taxied into the harbor and took off. "I did not know when we came out [of the water], and looked over the side to see if I was right. The surprise of it seemed to stun me. Not that I lost consciousness, but I was literally lost in amazement at the suddenness of it," remembered Miss Tarbell. Finally, the pilot brought the plane in for a smooth water landing, and taxied up to the landing ramp to allow his passenger to disembark. But she remained seated, transfixed by her first flying experience. "I do not know how long I sat in the boat not realizing that I must get out, so overwhelmed was I at the wonder of the thing . . . so supremely superior to any other emotion that I had ever experienced."[17]

Even observers of the new flying machines overhead found the sight to be a stunning experience. When Walter Brookins flew a Wright plane from Chicago to Springfield in 1910, a writer for the Chicago *Record Herald* reported that the plane drew out great crowds at every town along the way, as train whistles and fire sirens maintained a continuous exultant din along the entire 190-mile route. In baroque prose that captured the excitement of an era, he wrote:

> The sky-gazers looked on in astonishment as the great artificial bird bore down the heavens. . . . Wonderment, surprise, absorption were written on every visage . . . a machine of travel that combined the speed of the locomotive with the comfort of the automobile, and in addition, sped

17. John B. Huber, "Psychology of Aviation," *Scientific American*, CIII (October 29, 1910), p. 338; Ida M. Tarbell, "Flying—A Dream Come True," *American Magazine*, LXXVI (November, 1913), p. 66. The first American aviatrix, Harriet Quimby, learned to fly in 1911, and became the first woman to fly the English Channel. Sixteen-year-old Katherine Stinson became a pilot in 1912, joining several other female fliers of the pre-war era.

through an element until now navigated only by the feathered kind. It was, in truth, the poetry of motion, and its appeal to the imagination was evident in every upturned face.[18]

There can be little doubt that many Americans were indeed awed by this new flying contraption, and were beginning to ponder where it might lead. In a quaint rhyme of 1910, the poet wondered about the airplane's use in war, but eventually concluded on a positive note:

Brilliant, dashing, winged thing
    Moving there across the sky,
What new message do you bring
    Unto mankind as you fly?

Swift you cleave the vibrant air,
    Now you fly and now you float,
Life itself you seem to share —
    Are you bird or are you boat?

What new era do you bring
    Speading to us through the years?
Hark! Your motor seems to sing
    With the music of the spheres!

Shall mad hosts who go to war
    Look to you for deadly skill?
Will you only sing and soar
    So that men may maim and kill?

Rather may you skim the seas
    And go whirring near and far,
Fly to yonder Pleiades,
    Visit moon and evening star.

Waft young lovers through the air,
    Ply them straight to Heaven's own door;
Ride on sunbeams bright and fair,
    Chase you cloudlets at your fore.

Go where gods in laughter sit,
    Take us where life is but kind,
Seek where elves and fairies flit —
    Some new Eden for us to find.

Tiny airship, light and strong,
    Lifting upward to the sky,
Like a joyous, rising song,
    You shall teach our souls to fly!

18. News clippings from "Aeronautical Archives (1783-1962), American Institute of Aeronautics and Astronautics," in Manuscripts Division, Library of Congress, Boxes 9 and 270. Cited hereafter as LC/AIAA.

As romantic as the flying machine might seem to poets and enthusiastic crowds, the airplane was still a tricky thing to fly. The early products of the Wrights and others were controllable but unstable, and pilots preferred to go aloft early in the morning or late in the afternoon when the air was at its calmest. Even then, they were carefully watching flags and smoke plumes, and anxiously sticking wet fingers above their heads to test the breeze. This situation created problems. When a county fair listed an airplane flight at 2:30 PM, the crowd insisted on seeing one, and if a pilot demurred, he was considered a fraud. Stalling for time one breezy day, Beckwith Havens meandered around the flying field, looking, he said, for dangerous gopher holes. The local sheriff suddenly pulled up beside him in a horse-drawn buckboard, ordered him to get in, and unceremoniously hauled him back to the grandstand to start flying as specified. Such pressures led to the deaths of many fliers. Frank Coffyn was one of four men who signed two-year flying contracts with the Wright Exhibition Company, and he was the only one who lived to fulfill it. Pilots read daily newspapers with dread suspense, since nearly every week brought news of a fellow airman's demise.[19]

The fatality rate was compounded of pressures to fly when conditions were marginal, ill-conceived stunts and maneuvers, and sheer carelessness. Ralph Johnstone, for example, was an ex-vaudeville performer who joined the Wright Exhibition Company as a pilot. He and many like him flew for thrills and money, and they literally flew until their airplane's wings dropped off. After superficially repairing a damaged wing, it collapsed in mid-air, and Johnstone plunged to his death in full view of a large crowd at Denver in 1910. These disasters daunted neither the fliers nor the growing crowds. The lurking element of disaster morbidly attracted more spectators. General "Hap" Arnold, who had visited the 1910 Belmont meet as a young lieutenant, recalled the ghoulish expectations of many onlookers: "The crowd. . .gaped at the wonders, the exhibits of planes from home and abroad, secure in the knowledge that nowhere on earth, between now and suppertime, was there such a good chance of seeing somebody break his neck." For many Americans, the romantic view of aviation began to turn sour, expressed in the following jingle of the pre-World War I era:

There was an old woman who lived in a hangar
She had many children who raised such a clangor
    That some she gave poison, and some aeroplanes,
And all of them died with terrible pains.[20]

Before long, crowds began to tire of steep turns, spiral dives, and other gyrations. An aerial circus had been the best way to attract crowds and draw a paid attendance, but dwindling gates caused promoters to look for new

19. Grover Loening, "Fifty Years of Flying Progress," Smithsonian Institution, *Annual Report* (1954), p. 209; interviews of Milling, Coffyn, James Doolittle, and Beckwith Havens, OHC.

20. "Johnstone's Fate and Its Lesson," *Scientific American*, CIII (December 3, 1910), p. 434; Arnold *Mission*, p. 14; interviews of Havens and Benjamin Foulois, OHC; Limerick from LC/ AIAA, Box 270.

means to turn a profit at a time when pressure was building for alternative ways to demonstrate airplanes. In several articles, the *Scientific American* deplored the deaths of fliers due to stunting and asked for more competition such as long-distance flights in order to give the public a chance to ". . . contrast the aeroplane as a practical means of transport across country with the aeroplane as a provider of sensational amusement." This suggestion became a trend, and Calbraith P. Rodgers, who had received training at the Wrights flying school, completed the first transcontinental flight in 1911. Rodgers' plane, a modified Wright EX type, was named the *Vin Fiz*, after the product of an enterprising soft drink company who helped sponsor the effort. Rodgers' main interest was the Hearst newspaper prize of $50,000 for the first coast-to-coast flight within 30 days. Heading west for California, he took off on September 17, accompanied by a special train carrying spare parts. Traveling as wind, weather, and daylight allowed, and after recuperating from injuries sustained in an intervening crack-up, it took 49 days of flying and nearly three months elapsed time to complete the trip to the coast. In spite of the time and difficulties involved, it *was* the first time anyone had flown coast-to-coast, and at least proved that it could be done. Encouraged, the *Scientific American* predicted regular transcontinental passenger and air mail flights in the future.[21]

The odyssey of the *Vin Fiz* prompted similar promotional ventures, frequently disappointing and sometimes fatal. Rodgers himself died in a crash within four months of completing his transcontinental effort. One of the persistent criticisms of aeronautics in the prewar era was the death toll, not only of the inexperienced novice lured by cash awards for cross-country records, but also of the early birdmen and exhibition flyers. Many observers, while acknowledging some usefulness of stunting, remained concerned. Glenn Curtiss felt that many pilots had advanced aviation by maneuvers demonstrating the capabilities of the airplane. Nevertheless, Curtiss castigated the "fancy flying" and "spectacular gyrations" of some flyers as unnecessary and foolhardy. Wilbur Wright said that "legitimate fancy flying" could be safe, for it gave valuable experience in handling aircraft and becoming accustomed to flying, but he was strongly opposed to extreme fancy flying merely for thrills.[22]

Journalistic criticism continued to mount. The Boston *Transcript* declared that "circus stunts . . . [must] be separated in the public mind from aviation proper, either as a sport or a business." The widely read magazine *Current Literature* reprinted a cartoon from the Chicago *Tribune* entitled, "The Sirens of the Sky." It depicted an aviator being tempted by sky-sirens offering "prize money," "glory," "fame," and "applause," with Death seen lurking just over the

---

21. "Aeroplane Touring vs. Exhibition Flying," *Scientific American*, CV (August 26, 1911), p. 182; "Retrospect of the Year 1911: Aviation, "*Scientific American*, CV (December 30, 1911), pp. 591, 602.

22. Curtiss, *Curtiss Aviation Book*, p. 163; "Wilbur Wright on Altitude and Fancy Flying," *Aero*, I (December 17, 1910), p. 3.

pilot's shoulder. An accompanying cartoon, from the New York *Herald,* featured the Grim Reaper, with scythe and hour glass, wearing a sandwichboard ad emblazoned, "Sensational Acrobatic Aerial Performances for the Amusement of the Public. All the Most Dangerous Feats of the Air Men." Rogers subtitled his cartoon, "The Kind of Show that Kills the Sport." In 1911, after two seasons of aerial show business, the Wrights retired from flying exhibitions with distaste, although Curtiss and other troupes continued to play county fairs and other local festivals across the country.[23]

It was during this period that the airplane was first used in a practical demonstration as a freight carrier; but compared to the excitement of assorted aerial stunts and endurance flights, the significance of transporting man-made goods by air was almost lost. In November, 1910, a department store in Columbus, Ohio made arrangements with the Wrights to have a bolt of silk, to be cut up for souvenirs, flown up from Dayton by Phil Parmalee. In the aftermath of this first air express, the newspapers of Columbus paused to assess the significance of the event. As produced and presented by a professional air-showman like Roy Knabenshue, the flight was, not surprisingly, a drama of high adventure, and this is how it remained for many who witnessed it. An editorial in the Columbus *Journal* on the following morning still breathed the excitement of spectacle. "Our news columns will tell all about the flight," the paper proclaimed, "but the poetry of it, the romance of it, dwells in the mind like a dream, which cannot be expressed."

Yet, stirred in with awe of the episode, there was a dash of realism. It was recognized that Parmalee's trip was more than just a stunt, that the transfer of the pieces of silk by air had added importance beyond their value as mere souvenirs of an exciting flight. The fact remained that an airplane had not only flown from Dayton to Columbus; an airplane carrying a man and a cargo had bested the crack "Big Four" railroad express between the two cities. "The idea of a man flying up here from Dayton—where is your railroad train, your traction, your automobile now?" the *Journal* demanded. "Relegated to bygone days, along with the stage coach and the canal boat." Breaking away from a rhapsodic description of Parmalee's arrival, one reporter paused to give a nod to "the marvels of aerial navigation and aerial freight transportation" before allowing his fancy to take flight again. As the more pragmatic editors of the *Scientific American* observed, the additional use of a car to whisk the silk from landing field to sales counter constituted a "striking demonstration of the conjunctive use of the aeroplane and the automobile in the delivery of mail and express."[24]

Additional efforts to put the airplane to practical uses followed. There were experimental airmail flights in 1911, and innovative, if short-lived, passenger

23. "Immorality of Aviation," *Current Literature,* L (February, 1911), pp. 126-27; Lloyd Morris and Kendall Smith, *Ceiling Unlimited* (New York, 1953), pp. 115-19; Kelly, *Wright Brothers,* pp. 282-83.

24. Bilstein, "Putting Aircraft to Work," pp. 256-57; "The First Aeroplane Express," *Scientific American,* CIII (December 10, 1910), p. 464.

services in California and Florida two years later. Still, many people, even informed individuals, viewed the future of aviation with a jaundiced eye. In 1915, Professor Jerome Hunsaker, who taught one of the first courses in aeronautical engineering at the Massachusetts Institute of Technology, received an inquiry from Glenn Martin, who wanted to employ an aero engineer for his new airplane company. Donald Douglas, one of Hunsaker's recently graduated students, was looking for a job. Douglas said he was interested, but Hunsaker thought he would be better off in mechanical engineering. "This airplane business will never amount to very much," Hunsaker cautioned him.[25]

But times were changing. In Europe, intense national rivalries had flared into open hostilities during the summer of 1914, and for the first time, airplanes and airmen were joined in combat. On the eve of America's entry into the war in 1917, Orville Wright still saw a benign future for aviation, predicting business trips, air cargo, and an air mail service. Following the American declaration of hostilities, he endorsed bombing German munition production sites, and advocated air supremacy to keep enemy air reconnaissance suppressed. In November, 1918, as the conflict neared its end, he wrote hopefully to a friend: "The Aeroplane has made war so terrible that I do not believe any country will again care to start a war."[26]

Before World War I, nations had relied on geographical distance or natural barriers to protect their armies, population, and industry. The advent of air power changed all that. Although America was somewhat slower than other nations to grasp the new implications of the evolving age of flight, aviation definitely entered the public consciousness. Out of the war, a struggling aviation industry began to grow, and the airplane was utilized in a growing number of practical ways, including aerial photography and crop dusting. The National Advisory Committee for Aeronautics, founded in 1915, became one of the world's leading aeronautical research organizations in the postwar era. By 1925, a regularly scheduled airmail service linked the Atlantic and Pacific seaboards; U.S. Navy flying boats had crossed the Atlantic; and a pair of U.S. Army planes had circumnavigated the world by air. Such progress could not fail to impress the American public.

In 1935, reaching for a proper perspective on these and other momentous events, Mark Sullivan completed the last of a comprehensive and richly detailed six-volume study of America, entitled *Our Times: The United States, 1900-1925*. Reviewing the first quarter of the twentieth century, Sullivan commented on the impact of aeronautics on the public mind. Before the turn of the century, Sullivan reminded his readers, the impossibility of human flight had been accepted as axiomatic—an unalterable fact of nature like the

25. Interview of Donald Douglas, OHC.

26. Burton J. Hendrick. "The Safe and Useful Airplane: An Interview with Orville Wright," *Harper's Magazine*, CXXXIV (April, 1917, pp. 609-16; O. Wright To C. M. Hitchcock (June 21, 1917), and O. Wright to Dr. Wallace C. Sabine (November 7, 1918), in Marvin W. McFarland, ed., *The Papers of Wilbur and Orville Wright* (New York, 1953), vol. II, pp. 1104-05, 1121.

progression of winter and summer, the law of gravity, and the inevitability of death. An affirmation of God and the repudiation of flight contained the same unassailable, elementary truth. Thinking the unthinkable, the Wright brothers achieved the impossible in 1903. If flight were possible, Sullivan asked, what other immutabilities might be liable to change? The achievement of flight was a landmark in freeing ordinary individuals from the limitations of the status quo, stimulating the free inquiry of the intellect. "Of all the agencies that influenced man's mind," Sullivan wrote, "that made the average man of 1925 intellectually different from him of 1900, by far the greatest was the sight of a human being in an airplane."[27]

Such was the legacy of the Wright brothers.

27. Sullivan, *Our Times*, II, pp. 556-57.

ROGER E. BILSTEIN is Associate Professor of History at the University of Houston at Clear Lake City. During the 1977-78 academic year, he held an appointment as Visiting Curator of the Department of Science and Technology, National Air and Space Museum. He received his Ph.D. in history from the Ohio State University in 1965, and is editor of *Fundamentals of Aviation and Space Technology* (1974), author of *The Saturn Management Concept* (1974), as well as articles and conference papers on various aspects of aviation and space. He has written NASA's official history of the Saturn launch vehicles and is presently at work on a historical survey of American aviation. He received a writer's citation from the Aviation/Space Writers Association in 1974, and was the recipient of the Robert H. Goddard Historical Essay Award for 1977, presented by the National Space Club.

Recollections and Reflections

PAUL E. GARBER

As I walk through our National Air and Space Museum, I enjoy many memories of days spent obtaining aircraft for the Smithsonian Institution. I have delightful recollections of meeting the individuals who made and flew them; at times, they assisted me in bringing them here and assembling them and preparing labels for exhibits. Now I have the additional thrill of seeing these vehicles beautifully exhibited by an excellent team which has taken over where I left off. I recall the words of the British ambassador at the ceremony when we received the Wright brothers' Kitty Hawk aircraft. He described it as "The most magnificent example of the audacity of man."

I was not at Kill Devil Hill to see Orville Wright make that most epochal of all pioneer flights, though I wish I had been. But six years later I saw him piloting the Wright Military Flyer at Fort Myer, Virginia, and 39 years after that, I had the honor of bringing the first Wright "aeroplane" back home and installing it in the Smithsonian Institution's Arts and Industries Building. I also helped obtain our third Wright airplane — Calbraith Rodgers' *Vin Fiz.* My background greatly influenced my career. Born within a hundred yards of the ocean surf at Atlantic City, New Jersey, the first sounds I heard included the waves and wind. At age five I flew my first kite; one of my first toys was a jigsaw puzzle of an airship. I flew models, starting with one of the Wright Military Flyer, organized a model airplane club, and then, in 1915, I made and piloted a hang glider based on a scale model of a Chanute glider that I had seen on exhibit at the Smithsonian Institution. I received flight instruction in the Army during the First World War; the Armistice cut short my military career, and I did not solo until 1919 while an employee in the Postal Air Mail Service. I joined the Smithsonian in 1920, repairing artifacts for display, but always keeping my mind on aviation. I built scale models of historic aircraft, and this interest, plus the acquisition of the actual Fokker T-2, Douglas World Cruiser, Berliner Helicopter, and Lindbergh's *Spirit of St. Louis,* led to the establishment of a Section of Aeronautics and my connection with it—the roots of the present-day National Air and Space Museum.

One day an acquaintance visited the museum with Orville Wright; they had come to look at the Langley Aerodrome, and I had the pleasure of meeting the first man to make a powered, sustained, and controlled flight. Later, he assisted me in preparing an exhibit illustrating some of the accomplishments of his brother and himself. I saw him on many other occasions, and as I recall those times I only wish that I had asked him more quesitons! Regrettably he died on January 30, 1948. In November of that year, it was my privilege to help bring back the 1903 Flyer from England, where it had been on exhibit at the Science Museum since 1928, to the United States, for installation in the Smithsonian Institution.

It was shipped aboard the liner *Mauritania*. I was to meet the director of the Science Museum, who was accompanying the Kitty Hawk airplane across the Atlantic, when the liner *Mauritania* docked in New York. Through the courtesy of a former commanding officer, the Navy arranged for me to have a truck available to ferry the aircraft to Washington. As I arrived at the Customs House in New York, I was handed two messages. One read, "You must go to Halifax." The other intoned, "Call St. Peter." I thought that if I had to go to Halifax I would do well to call St. Peter first! I did so and learned that he was Aloysius St. Peter, in the public relations office of the Wright Aeronautical Corporation. He asked me if I could stop by their factory enroute to Washington so they could pay their respects to the Wright brothers and the Wright airplane; I quickly assented, and later we did stop on our way to the enshrinement at the Smithsonian. The other message came from the British Embassy: the captain of the *Mauritania* had learned of a dock strike in New York, and had decided to unload at Halifax. Off I went. From the window of the airplane I could see the *Mauritania* as it approached the harbor. I hurried to dockside after landing, met the director of the Science Museum and his wife, and arranged for the Royal Canadian Air Force to fly them to an honorary dinner in New York that evening being hosted by Grover Loening. Meantime, I hovered protectingly over the three boxes that contained aviation's greatest treasure — the Wright 1903 Flyer. How could I get this to Washington? In Halifax, I didn't even have a wheelbarrow.

Fortunately I had a friend in high places: Admiral Mel Pride, my old commanding officer from the Second World War. I went to the office of the American consul and phoned Admiral Pride, asking him if he had a ship that could come and get me and the Flyer. "Good God, Garber," he responded, "you think of the damndest things." Then he said he'd see what could be done. I waited anxiously. Several hours later he called back: the escort carrier U.S.S. *Palau* was finishing maneuvers off Argentia, and would proceed to Halifax to pick up the Wright Flyer. Indeed, as a Commander, U.S. Naval Reserve, I would be considered on active duty while aboard. With things working out at last, I arranged for room and board; I had not dressed for November in Nova Scotia, had only a small overnight kit, and little money.

On the second day after my arrival in Halifax, I spent from morning until late evening at a dockyard shed, staying close to the Flyer. There was one totally unexpected and delightful break. Towards noon, I was standing at the wharf-edge, looking toward the sea for any sign of the *Palau*. Up stepped an impressive-looking gentleman. Without introducing himself, he asked if I was the custodian of the Wright Flyer. I admitted that I was. As we chatted he asked me to join him for lunch, and we went to a nearby hotel. I still did not know his name, but as we entered the hotel, I noticed that many persons obviously recognized him—and the waiter was very deferential. Soon after we were seated he was called to the telephone. He returned and apologized, saying that "Dr. Bell was often annoyed when his invention interrupted something he was trying to do." Then my mind clicked: my mysterious host was none other than the Honorable John A. D. McCurdy, a member of Dr. Alexander Graham Bell's Aerial Experiment Association, which Bell had founded in 1907. In 1908 McCurdy had designed the *Silver Dart*, the first airplane to fly in Canada, which he piloted on February 23, 1909. A close associate of pioneer Glenn Curtiss, he had risen to Lieutenant Governor of Nova Scotia — and now I could participate in the conversation with more appreciation.

On the third day the *Palau* entered harbor, to the accompanyment of a tumultous salute from every warship in harbor—no, not for the carrier, but in honor of the birth of Charles, the Prince of Wales! As the *Palau* could not dock where I waited, I arranged for a crane to place the three boxes containing the Wright Flyer aboard a lighter, which a tug then pushed alongside the carrier. I rigged a coil of line to each box, and we hoisted them aboard the *Palau*. The voyage down the East Coast was anticlimatic and pleasant. The carrier docked at Bayonne, New Jersey, and a large Navy truck labeled "Operation Homecoming" pulled up to the dock to ferry the Flyer to Washington, manned by a Smithsonian crew. A detachment of sailors presented arms, and we began our journey south. It was more like a triumphal procession; we stopped at the Wright Aeronautical Corporation, and at nearly every town or city we had a police escort. We spent a night at the Philadelphia Navy Yard, and continued on to Washington the next day.

A Smithsonian reception committee greeted us at the steps on the Freer Gallery of Art, and when the ceremony ended, I took the boxes to the Arts and Industries Building, breathing a deep sigh of relief that this immortal treasure was at home at last. I have other memories, too, such as Charles Lindbergh's reply when I told him I planned to move the *Spirit of St. Louis* so that I could suspend the Wright Flyer in front of it: he answered that of the many honors he had received, one of the highest would be the *Spirit of St. Louis* sharing the same hall as the Wright Flyer.

Today, in the new National Air and Space Museum, they again share the same hall. I recall the excellent help of Stanley Potter. We worked together in the rafters of the hall attaching the pulley tackle and cables for raising the Flyer. When I had ordered the cables, the manufacturer had refused payment; it was their privilege, the company's officials said, to furnish them. The Science Museum had carefully tagged every part and its relationship to other parts. Together with several fellow-members of The Early Birds of Aviation, some of whom had worked on and flown Wright airplanes during their heyday, I shared the honor of working on the 1903 Flyer. We corrected any evidence of deterioration. (When it was moved from the Arts and Industries Building to the new National Air and Space Museum, a move that necessitated disassembly and packing, every care was again taken by museum craftsmen to ensure the accuracy of reassembly and preservation.) The ceremonies dedicating the aircraft on December 17, 1948 were most impressive; at long last, the Wright 1903 Flyer was home. It had returned from across the ocean to join its fellow pioneers, the Wright 1909 Military Flyer, and the *Vin Fiz*. They, too, arouse other recollections, and I often pause during my tours of our exhibits to admire them. I can look through the window of a modern jet airliner and see the Wright aircraft flying along, changing the course of history.

PAUL E. GARBER is Historian Emeritus and Ramsey Fellow of the National Air and Space Museum. A native of Atlantic City, New Jersey, Mr. Garber attended schools in New Jersey and the District of Columbia, and the University of Maryland. He became interested in aviation in 1909 when he saw Orville Wright fly at Ft. Myer. After working with the Air Mail Service, he joined the Smithsonian Institution in 1920. During the Second World War, Mr. Garber served as a Commander, U.S. Naval Reserve. He was appointed the first Curator of the National Air Museum following his return from military service. Born in 1899, Mr. Garber was required to retire upon reaching the mandatory retirement age of 70, but was awarded honorary status as Historian Emeritus and Ramsey Fellow. A member of The Early Birds of Aviation and the Air Mail Pioneers, Mr. Garber has received numerous awards and decorations, including the Gold Medal for Exceptional Service of the Smithsonian Institution.

The Wright Brothers:
A Photographic Essay

The Inventors of the Airplane

Wilbur Wright (1867-1912)
National Air And Space Museum (NASM)

Orville Wright (1871-1948) *NASM*

The Wright brothers lived in this house, at 7 Hawthorn Street, Dayton, Ohio, when they began their flight studies. In 1937, the house was moved to Henry Ford's Greenfield Village Museum at Dearborn, Michigan. *NASM*

Kitty Hawk: The Early Years

The brothers first flew this machine, their 1900 glider, as a tethered kite. This biplane kite-glider spanned 17 feet and had a wing area of 165 square feet, with a canard elevator for pitch control and wing-warping for roll (lateral) control. Only a few piloted tethered and free flights were made; most flights were unmanned.
William J. Hammer Collection, NASM

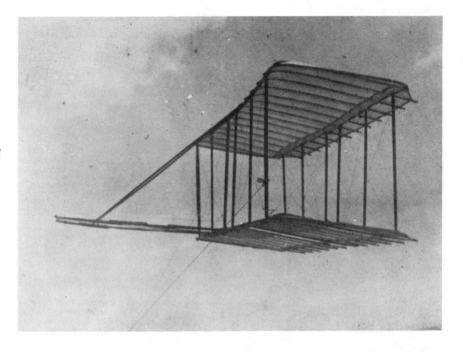

After examining Weather Bureau reports to determine a suitable location for flight testing their designs, the Wright brothers set up camp at Kitty Hawk, North Carolina, an isolated sandy beach with good winds, in September 1900.
Hammer Collection. NASM

A year later, in 1901, the brothers built a larger
glider spanning 22 feet, with a wing area of 290
square feet. During July and August of 1901, they
tested this glider in flight, but found that the
machine did not perform to their satisfaction, even
though they completed glides up to 389 feet. They
returned to Dayton determined to undertake detailed aerodynamic research. *Hammer Collection,
NASM*

Scientific Experimentation

No mere tinkerers, the Wrights undertook an intensive aerodynamic research program between September 1901 and August 1902. Here is a rudimentary device they used to measure lift. It consisted of a wheel affixed ahead of the handlebars of a bicycle. The wheel had two surfaces mounted on it, one being a flat plate for reference purposes, and the other being an experimental airfoil (wing cross-section). As one of the brothers pedaled, the lift generated by the experimental airfoil would overcome the resistance of the flat plate, causing the wheel to turn. *M. P. Baker Collection, NASM*

A more satisfactory device was this wind tunnel, shown here in replica form, which the brothers used for more exacting and detailed measurements. Their pioneering wind tunnel tests enabled them to evaluate previous air pressure tables compiled by other experimenters. As a result, the Wrights rejected these earlier efforts as inaccurate and misleading, and developed their own tables to use in the design of their flight vehicles. *Baker Collection, NASM*

This small wind tunnel balance enabled the Wrights to measure the lift and drag of various experimental airfoils. *Baker Collection, NASM*

62

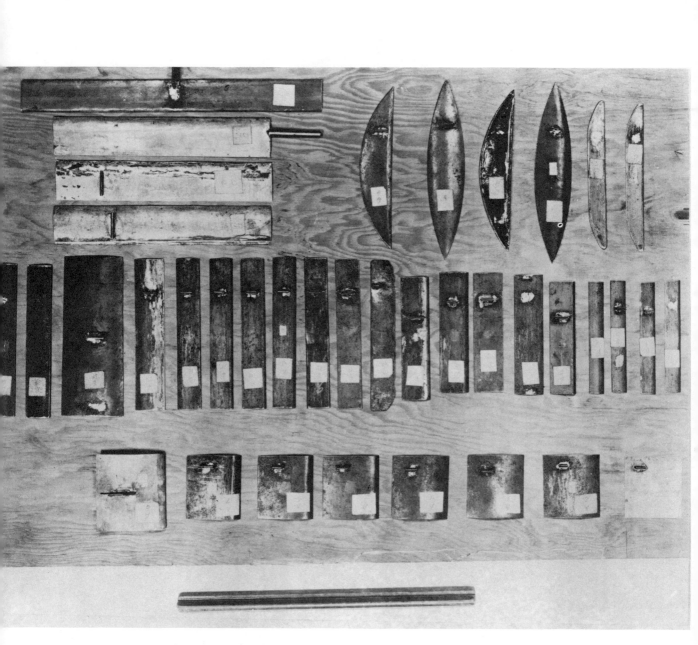

A sampling of the various airfoils
tested in the Wright's tunnel; their
careful experimentation placed them
at the forefront of serious flight researchers. *Baker Collection, NASM*

Return to Kitty Hawk: Tests of the 1902 Glider

Below:
As a result of their wind tunnel research, the Wrights developed the 1902 glider, a biplane spanning over 32 feet, and having a wing area of 305 square feet. It had a canard elevator, wing warping, and, significantly, a double-surface fixed rudder to improve stability during turns. Here it is seen being flown pilotless, as a kite. *Hammer Collection, NASM*

Wilbur Wright piloting the 1902 glider during its initial flight tests, September 1902. *Hammer Collection, NASM*

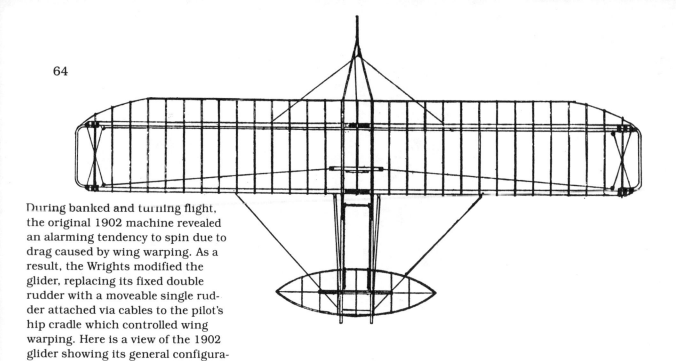

During banked and turning flight, the original 1902 machine revealed an alarming tendency to spin due to drag caused by wing warping. As a result, the Wrights modified the glider, replacing its fixed double rudder with a moveable single rudder attached via cables to the pilot's hip cradle which controlled wing warping. Here is a view of the 1902 glider showing its general configuration as modified with the single rudder. *NASM*

Orville Wright being launched for a flight in the 1902 (modified) glider, October 1902. *NASM*

The 1902 (modified) glider just after launch from the dunes at Kitty Hawk. *NASM*

The 1902 (modified) glider banking. The wing warping action for lateral control is readily apparent. The 1902 (modified) glider was the first winged vehicle capable of effective three-axis control — control in roll, pitch, and yaw. *Hammer Collection, NASM*

The 1902 (modified) glider in free flight. *Hammer Collection, NASM*

Triumph at Kitty Hawk

The Accomplishment of the World's First Powered, Sustained, and Controlled Flight.

During the summer of 1903, the Wright brothers built the famous Wright Flyer of 1903. They returned to Kitty Hawk with the new aircraft in September 1903, beginning flight trials in mid-December. *NASM-U.S. Army Air Forces.*

One major obstacle in their path was the lack of a suitable powerplant for the aircraft. The Wrights designed their own engine, a four-cylinder piston engine weighing 179 lbs. and producing 12 horsepower at 1,090 rpm. The engine drove two wooden pusher propellers. *NASM*

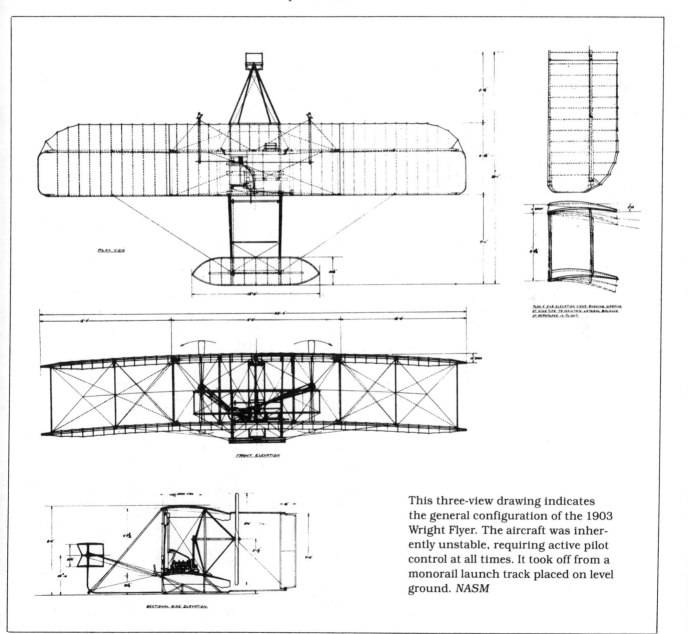

Propeller development was another
critical area that could have slowed
the Wrights' work. As a result of
careful research, they produced
highly efficient propellers. Here is
one of the propellers used on the
1903 Flyer. *NASM*

PLAN VIEW

PLAN & END ELEVATION VIEWS SHOWING WARPING
OF WING TIPS TO MAINTAIN LATERAL BALANCE
OF AEROPLANE IN FLIGHT.

FRONT ELEVATION

SECTIONAL SIDE ELEVATION.

This three-view drawing indicates
the general configuration of the 1903
Wright Flyer. The aircraft was inherently unstable, requiring active pilot
control at all times. It took off from a
monorail launch track placed on level
ground. *NASM*

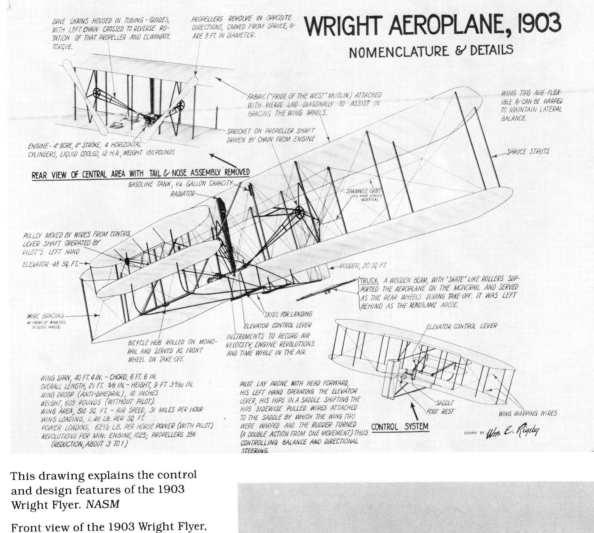

WRIGHT AEROPLANE, 1903
NOMENCLATURE & DETAILS

DRIVE CHAINS HOUSED IN TUBING - GUIDES, WITH LEFT CHAIN CROSSED TO REVERSE ROTATION OF THAT PROPELLER AND ELIMINATE TORQUE.

PROPELLERS REVOLVE IN OPPOSITE DIRECTIONS, CARVED FROM SPRUCE, & ARE 8 FT. IN DIAMETER.

FABRIC ("PRIDE OF THE WEST" MUSLIN) ATTACHED WITH WEAVE LAID DIAGONALLY TO ASSIST IN BRACING THE WING PANELS.

WING TIPS ARE FLEXIBLE & CAN BE WARPED TO MAINTAIN LATERAL BALANCE.

ENGINE - 4" BORE, 4" STROKE, 4 HORIZONTAL CYLINDERS, LIQUID COOLED, 12 H.P., WEIGHT 180 POUNDS

SPROCKET ON PROPELLER SHAFT DRIVEN BY CHAIN FROM ENGINE

SPRUCE STRUTS

REAR VIEW OF CENTRAL AREA WITH TAIL & NOSE ASSEMBLY REMOVED

GASOLINE TANK, ¼ GALLON CAPACITY
RADIATOR

SPANWISE GUYS TO KEEP STRUTS VERTICAL

PULLEY MOVED BY WIRES FROM CONTROL LEVER SHAFT OPERATED BY PILOT'S LEFT HAND
ELEVATOR - 48 SQ. FT.

RUDDER, 20 SQ. FT.

TRUCK A WOODEN BEAM, WITH "SKATE" LIKE ROLLERS SUPPORTED THE AEROPLANE ON THE MONORAIL AND SERVED AS THE REAR WHEELS DURING TAKE-OFF. IT WAS LEFT BEHIND AS THE AEROPLANE AROSE.

WIRE BRACING AT FRONT OF WING CELL IN OUTER PANELS.

SKIDS FOR LANDING
ELEVATOR CONTROL LEVER
INSTRUMENTS TO RECORD AIR VELOCITY, ENGINE REVOLUTIONS AND TIME WHILE IN THE AIR.

ELEVATOR CONTROL LEVER

BICYCLE HUB ROLLED ON MONORAIL AND SERVED AS FRONT WHEEL ON TAKE-OFF.

WING SPAN, 40 FT. 4 IN. - CHORD, 6 FT. 6 IN.
OVERALL LENGTH, 21 FT. 3/8 IN. - HEIGHT, 9 FT. 3 5/32 IN.
WING DROOP (ANTI-DIHEDRAL), 10 INCHES
WEIGHT, 605 POUNDS (WITHOUT PILOT).
WING AREA, 510 SQ. FT. - AIR SPEED, 31 MILES PER HOUR
WING LOADING, 1.46 LB. PER SQ. FT.
POWER LOADING, 62½ LB. PER HORSE POWER (WITH PILOT)
REVOLUTIONS PER MIN: ENGINE, 1025; PROPELLERS 356
(REDUCTION, ABOUT 3 TO 1)

PILOT LAY PRONE WITH HEAD FORWARD, HIS LEFT HAND OPERATING THE ELEVATOR LEVER, HIS HIPS IN A SADDLE. SHIFTING THE HIPS SIDEWISE PULLED WIRES ATTACHED TO THE SADDLE BY WHICH THE WING TIPS WERE WARPED AND THE RUDDER TURNED (A DOUBLE ACTION FROM ONE MOVEMENT) THUS CONTROLLING BALANCE AND DIRECTIONAL STEERING.

SADDLE
FOOT REST
WING WARPING WIRES
CONTROL SYSTEM

DRAWN BY Wm. E. Rigsby

This drawing explains the control and design features of the 1903 Wright Flyer. *NASM*

Front view of the 1903 Wright Flyer, taken at Kitty Hawk. *NASM*

Side view of the 1903 Wright Flyer, also at Kitty Hawk. *Hammer Collection, NASM*

The pilot's controls on the 1903 Wright Flyer. The pilot moved the hip cradle from side to side for lateral control (the hip cradle was also interconnected to the rudder), and the handle in left-center foreground for elevator (pitch) control. A French-built anemometer used for airspeed measurement is visible, mounted on the vertical wing strut in front of the engine; it was sent to the brothers by pioneer Octave Chanute. Note the engine control affixed to the wing below and to the right of the anemometer on the wing strut. *NASM*

December 14, 1903: The 1903 Wright Flyer is readied for its first flight trials. Pilot Wilbur Wright prepares to take off. *NASM*

Just after lift-off, however, he noses up too steeply and the machine stalls, landing heavily and sustaining minor damage. Repairs take until the afternoon of December 16 to complete. Now it is Orville Wright's turn. *NASM*

On December 17, 1903, at 10:35 a.m., the era of powered flight dawns, a triumph of flight research that fulfilled the dream of centuries. Orville Wright takes off in the face of a 27 mile-per-hour wind, covers 120 feet, and remains aloft 12 seconds. It was the world's first powered, sustained, and controlled flight. Taken by John T. Daniels, one of the witnesses, using Orville's camera. *NASM*

Three more flights are made that historic day. Here it is the 1903 Flyer on its third trial, skimming the dunes. *NASM-Library of Congress*

On the fourth flight, Wilbur Wright takes off at noon, flies for 59 seconds, and covers 852 feet. During a hard landing, the elevator supports are broken, though the machine is not seriously damaged. Shortly after this photograph was taken, however, a gust of wind rolls the 1903 Flyer over and over, badly damaging it, and ending the trials for that year. Jubilant with their success, the brothers return to Dayton. *NASM-Library of Congress*

Subsequently, the 1903 Wright Flyer was exhibited at various institutions. Here is shown at the Massachusetts Institute of Technology in 1916 . . . *NASM*

. . . and at the Science Museum, South Kensington, London, where it was on exhibit from 1928 to 1948 . . . *NASM*

and, finally, at the Smithsonian Institution, Washington, D.C., where it has been since 1948. *NASM*

The Huffman Prairie Years

In 1904, the Wrights began testing a new aircraft, the 1904 Wright Flyer II, at Huffman Prairie, an 87 acre pasture located 8 miles east of Dayton. It resembled the earlier 1903 machine, but had a more powerful engine and less camber (curve) to the wings. The Wrights introduced a novel weight-and-derrick to "catapult" the aircraft on takeoff, later adopting this method for launching their subsequent aircraft as well. The 1904 Flyer retained interlinked warp and rudder controls, and completed the world's first circling flight on September 20, 1904, piloted by Wilbur Wright. It was scrapped in 1905. *NASM-The Henry Ford Museum*

In 1905, the Wrights introduced their first practical powered airplane, the Wright Flyer III. This aircraft is shown just after take-off from Huffman Prairie. *NASM-Library of Congress*

The 1905 Flyer III originally had its rudder and warp controls interconnected. As a result of further flight experience, however, they modified the machine so that its rudder and warp controls were separate, greatly increasing its controllability. It could bank, circle, and perform Figure Eights. On October 5, 1905, it set an endurance record of 38 minutes, during which it flew over 24 miles. *NASM-Library of Congress*

The historic 1905 Wright Flyer III was rebuilt and placed on exhibit at Carillon Park, Dayton, Ohio. *NASM-The National Cash Register Company*

1908: The Incredible Year

In 1908, the Wright brothers demonstrated their aircraft in Europe and to the United States government. Wilbur Wright journeyed to France to supervise construction of a French-built Wright Type A Flyer. On August 8, 1908, he made the first flight of this machine, shown here, at a small racecourse at Hunaudières, 5 miles south of Le Mans. The flight revolutionized European aviation, which had lain dormant since the turn of the century. "Who can now doubt that the Wrights have done all they claimed?" asked René Gasnier. "We are as children compared with the Wrights." Here the Type A is readied for flight. *NASM-U.S. Army Air Forces*

Meanwhile, in America, Orville Wright was preparing for government tests of another Wright Type A machine, the 1908 Military Flyer. The Wrights had earlier approached both the American and British governments in 1905, offering them their aircraft. Both governments had rebuffed their overtures. Finally, in December 1907, the U.S. Army Signal Corps had issued a specification for a flying machine capable of carrying two crewmen at 40 mph. Here is the Wrights' response to the specification, in which they agree to provide a machine for Signal Corps tests at a cost of $25,000. *NASM-U.S. National Archives*

On February 10, 1908, the Signal Corps responded with a contract to the Wrights for "One (1) heavier-than-air flying machine." *NASM-U.S. National Archives*

The Signal Corps requirement
stipulated that the machine be
capable of transport by a wagon.
Here the 1908 Military Flyer is
shown being drawn by automobile to
Ft. Myer, Virginia, for testing. Note
how the forward structure of the
aircraft folded easily for transport.
*NASM-Eastman Kodak. Photo by
C.H. Claudy*

Orville Wright started the Ft. Myer
tests on September 3, 1908. Here
Orville Wright readies the Flyer for a
flight on September 12, 1908, with
Maj. George O. Squier as passenger.
Maj. Squier, who held a doctorate
from Johns Hopkins University, later
became chief of the Signal Corps'
Aviation Section. Note the ground
crewman preparing to swing one of
the pusher propellers. *U.S.
Navy-U.S. National Archives*

Orville Wright and Maj. Squier in flight, September 12, 1908. On the Type A machines, the pilot — and passenger, if any — sat upright. *NASM. Photo by W.S. Clime*

Some things did not change. The Wrights still used a chain drive to rotate the propellers. Like the cavalryman seen eyeing this new contraption, the Army envisioned the mission of the airplane to be scouting and reconnaissance. *NASM*

78

Side view of the 1908 Military Flyer in flight. *NASM. Clime photo.*

The Wrights also still relied on dropping a weight from a derrick to pull a launch wire which, in turn, catapulted the Flyer into the air. *NASM*

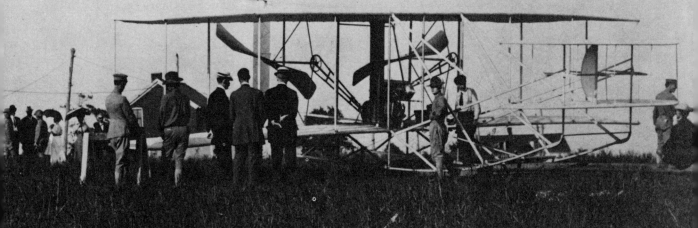

The 1908 Military Flyer passing overhead. *NASM. Clime photo.*

The 1908 Military Flyer showing its configuration, as seen from the rear. *NASM-Eastman Kodak. Claudy photo.*

In the late afternoon of September 17, 1908. Orville Wright takes off with Lt. Thomas Selfridge, who had earier worked with Dr. Alexander Graham Bell as a member of the Aerial Experiment Association . . . *NASM-Eastman Kodak. Claudy photo.*

. . . Tragedy strikes during the flight. The Flyer's right propeller fractures, setting up a vibration that causes it to strike and sever one of the rudder's bracing wires. The Flyer goes out of control. Due to Orville Wright's skillful pilotage, the machine recovers slightly before crashlanding; the pilot's actions save only his life, however. Lt. Selfridge suffers a fatal skull fracture, the first airman to die in the crash of a powered airplane. Orville is seriously injured, but recovers. The crash brings the trials to an end. *NASM-Library of Congress*

In January 1909, Wilbur Wright journeyed to Pau, France, where he flew from early February to late March. He is shown here at Pont Long, Pau, with a group of aviators and friends, and his sister Katharine. (Left to right) Louis Blériot, later the first to fly an airplane across the English Channel; Paul Tissandier; Capt. Lucas de Girardville; Wilbur Wright; Madame Hart O. Berg, who had earlier been the first woman passenger carried in an airplane when she flew with Wilbur Wright on October 7, 1908; Charles, Comte de Lambert; and Katharine Wright. Tissandier, Capt. Girardville, and the Comte de Lambert were all pupils of Wilbur Wright. *Hammer Collection, NASM*

In April 1909, Wilbur Wright gave demonstration and passenger flights at Centocelle, near Rome. Here he is seen flying low over Centocelle. Photographer Hart O. Berg took this photograph from a balloon. *Institute of the Aeronautical Sciences Collection, NASM*

1909: Orville Wright Returns to Ft. Myer

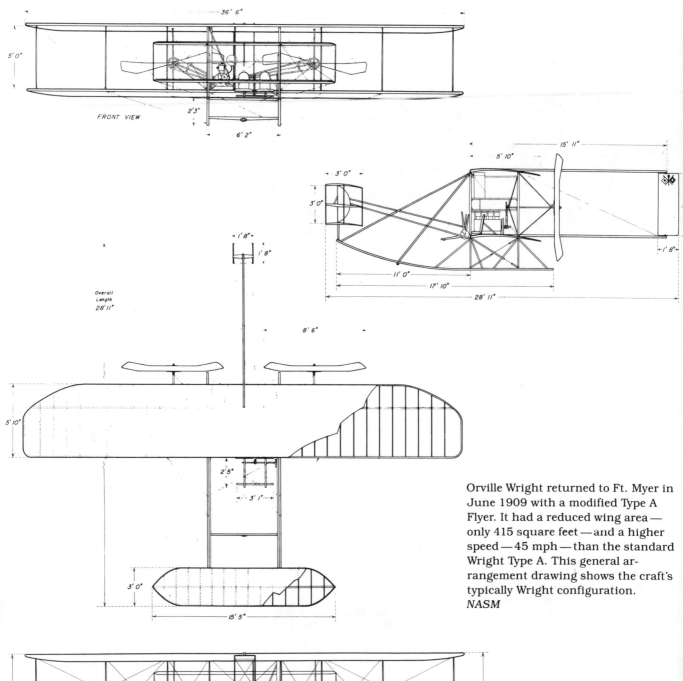

FRONT VIEW

Overall
Length
28' 11"

REAR VIEW

Orville Wright returned to Ft. Myer in June 1909 with a modified Type A Flyer. It had a reduced wing area—only 415 square feet—and a higher speed—45 mph—than the standard Wright Type A. This general arrangement drawing shows the craft's typically Wright configuration. *NASM*

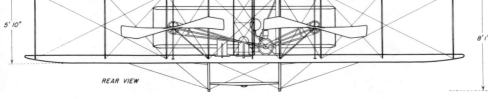

Here Wilbur Wright, in white shirt and derby, watches as Orville Wright (between skids) makes final adjustments to the aircraft before takeoff. The launch bar attached to the catapult cable is visible immediately behind Orville Wright. *NASM-Eastman Kodak. Claudy photo.*

The 1909 machine — commonly called the Signal Corps Flyer — flies low over Ft. Myer. *NASM. Clime photo.*

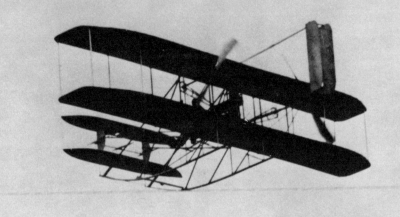

The 1909 Signal Corps Flyer in flight. Note the counterrotating propellers, a Wright hallmark. *NASM*

During the 1909 Ft. Myer trials, Orville Wright gave demonstration flights to interested Signal Corp officers. Here Lt. Frank Lahm — the first rated military pilot — rides as a passenger. *NASM. Clime photo, via A. W. Clime.*

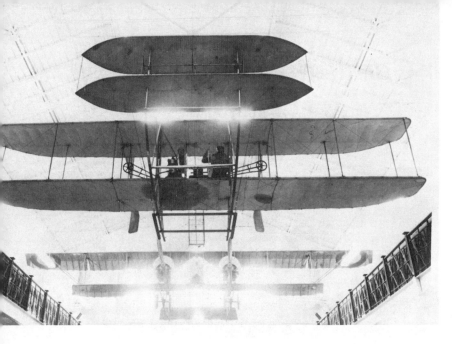

Following the 1909 trials, the 1909 Signal Corps Flyer was purchased by the Army. Eventually, it was transferred to the Smithsonian Institution, and it is now on exhibit in the National Air and Space Museum. It is the world's oldest military aircraft. *NASM*

Many dignitaries attended the 1909 Ft. Myer trials, including President William Howard Taft. President Taft —visible inside the tent, behind the tent pole—watches Orville in flight. *Aero Digest Collection, NASM*

1909: Flyers over Germany

In August 1909, Orville Wright went to Germany and made many flights over the next two months at Tempelhof and Potsdam. Here is the Flyer—a standard Type A—just after take off from the launching rail. *NASM via Heinz Nowarra*

Many dignitaries witnessed the flights in Germany, including the Empress of Germany, standing with this group, below the Flyer. This Flyer is on exhibit at the *Deutsches Museum. NASM Via Heinz Nowarra*

—and the Hudson

In September and October, 1909, Wilbur Wright made many flights witnessed by millions in connection with the Hudson-Fulton Celebration. On October 4, he flew 21 miles, up the Hudson River from Governors Island to beyond Grant's tomb, turned around, and flew back to the starting point. He installed a covered and water-tight canoe below the lower wing of the Flyer for emergency flotation in the event that the plane had to land on the river. Here the Flyer is shown after takeoff. *NASM*

Another view of the Flyer in flight on October 4; the flotation canoe is clearly visible. *NASM via Richard E. Gomez*

The Later Flyers

The Army quickly moved to establish aviation detachments within the Signal Corps. Here are the service's first machines in front of hangers at College Park, Maryland. Visible are two Wright aircraft (left) and two Curtiss airplanes (right). *NASM*

Another Wright military machine was the modified Type A of 1910 flown by the Signal Corps at Ft. Sam Houston. Note the innovations, including landing wheels added by Oliver Simmons (shown seated in pilot's seat), and the single front elevator. The upper surface of the front elevator had been removed and reinstalled behind the wing. *O. G. Simmons Collection, NASM*

Britain's Hon. C. S. Rolls flew this French-built Wright Type A across the Channel. It is shown here leaving for its return, on June 2, 1910. On July 12, Rolls was killed in the crash of this machine at Bournemouth. *NASM*

An unusual view of an experimental Wright modified Type A of 1911 equipped with a stabilizer attached to the rudder support frames. *NASM*

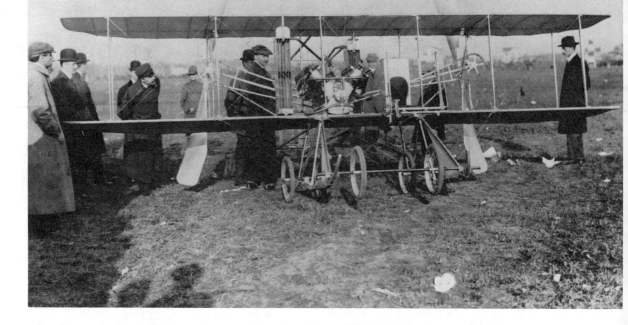

In 1910, the Wrights developed the Model R, also called the "Roadster" and, more popularly, the "Baby Wright." It was designed as a single-seat racer for setting speed and altitude records, and was equipped with a wheeled undercarriage. This is an even smaller version, the Baby Grand, powered by an 8 cylinder 60 hp piston engine. Orville Wright flew this aircraft at the 1910 Belmont Park Meet, attaining speeds over 70 mph. *NASM*

One of the best-known Wright aircraft was this modified Model EX of 1911, which Calbraith Perry Rodgers flew cross-country from Sheepshead Bay, New York, to Long Beach, California. Rodgers started his flight on September 17, and completed it on December 10. He made a total of 70 landings, and the plane accumulated a total flying time of 82 hours, 4 minutes. Popularly known as the *Vin Fiz*, this modified EX is now exhibited at the Smithsonian Institution's National Air and Space Museum. *NASM*

In October 1911, Orville Wright and British airman Alec Ogilvie flew a new Wright glider at the Kill Devil Hills, Kitty Hawk. This glider spanned 32 feet, and had a wing area of 300 square feet. At first, as shown here, the glider had a fixed vertical fin attached to a front strut. Later, as a result of flight experience, Wright moved it five feet forward. *NASM*

The modified 1911 glider soaring over Kitty Hawk. On
October 24, 1911, Orville set a world's soaring record of
9 minutes and 45 seconds. The record stood for a
decade. *NASM*

Orville Wright also experimented with floatplanes. After the death of
Wilbur Wright in 1912, Orville Wright modified a Model C Flyer to
produce the Model CH of 1913, the first Wright "hydroplane." The
Model CH had pontoons, and was tested on a deserted stretch of the
Miami River outside Dayton. The twin float arrangement shown here
was later changed to a large single float. *NASM*

Left: The 1911 glider —with the modified vertical
fin —after launch. *U.S. Air Force*

The Wright Factory

THE WRIGHT CO.

All the later Wright aircraft were built within this small factory located at Dayton, Ohio. License manufacture was also undertaken abroad. *NASM*

The General Assembly Department of the Wright factory. Workers are putting the finishing touches to a Model B Flyer. *NASM via Mrs. Ruth Jacobs*

GENERAL ASSEMBLY DEPARTMENT

An assembled Model B being readied for shipment. *NASM via S. Dunham*

Covering the wing of a Model B Flyer. *NASM via S. Dunham*

Stacked wing sections ready for joining with other subassemblies. *NASM-U. S. Army Air Corps*

The Wright production line, showing three Flyers in the process of assembly. *NASM via Roy Knabenshue*

In 1918, Orville Wright retired from piloting airplanes. He continued as the doyen of American aviation pioneers. He is shown here (in the center of the photo, smiling broadly, without a hat) at the dedication of Wright Field in October 1927. Orville Wright, the guest of honor, raised the flag at the ceremony, which marked the opening of one of the world's best-known research and development centers. *NASM-U.S. Army Air Forces Materiel Command*

Orville Wright continued to take an active part in aviation. He was a trustee of The Daniel Guggenheim Fund for the Promotion of Aeronautics (1926-1930), and is shown with other members of the fund at Port Washington, New York, on June 15, 1928. Shown (left to right) standing are: J. W. Miller; F. Trubee Davison; Elihu Root, Jr.; Hutchinson Cone; Charles Lindbergh; Harry Guggenheim, the fund president; Robert Millikan. Left to right, seated: John D. Ryan; Daniel Guggenheim, the fund's creator; Orville Wright; and William Durand. *Paul Iudica, Mason Studio, Port Washington, N.Y.*

Orville Wright always kept in close contact with the activities at Wright Field. Here he is shown in 1944 during the Second World War with Brig. Gen. Franklin O. Carroll, chief of the Army Air Corps' Engineering Division, headquartered at Wright Field. At the time this photograph was taken, the jet airplane was a reality, and supersonic flight lay a half-decade ahead. *NASM-U.S. Army Air Forces Materiel Command*

On April 26, 1944, Orville Wright flew as a passenger on a demonstration flight of a Lockheed C-69 Constellation transport at Wright Field. During the flight he took over the controls after takeoff, flying the Constellation from the co-pilot's position. *Lockheed Aircraft Corporation*

The Wright Brothers National Memorial, Big Kill Devil Hill, Kitty Hawk, North Carolina. *Susan J. Lowe*

Orville Wright: 'How We Made the First Flight'

On the tenth anniversary of the world's first powered, sustained, and controlled flight, Orville Wright published an account of the events and activities that surrounded that epochal achievement. His account appeared in the aviation journal Flying and The Aero Club of America Bulletin, *in the issue of December 1913, pp. 10-12, and 35-36. Because of the unique significance of this little-known primary account, it is reprinted here in full:*

The flights of the 1902 glider had demonstrated the efficiency of our system of maintaining equilibrium, and also the accuracy of the laboratory work upon which the design of the glider was based. We then felt that we were prepared to calculate in advance the performance of machines with a degree of accuracy that had never been possible with the data and tables possessed by our predecessors. Before leaving camp in 1902 we were already at work on the general design of a new machine which we proposed to propel with a motor.

Immediately upon our return to Dayton, we wrote to a number of automobile and motor builders, stating the purpose for which we desired a motor, and asking whether they could furnish one that would develop eight-brake horse power, with a weight complete not exceeding 200 pounds. Most of the companies answered that they were too busy with their regular business to undertake the building of such a motor for us; but one company replied that they had motors rated at 8 h.p., according to the French system of ratings, which weighed only 135 pounds, and that if *we thought* this motor would develop enough power for our purpose, they would be glad to sell us one. After an examination of the particulars of this motor, from which we learned that it had but a single cylinder of 4 inch bore and 5 inch stroke, we were afraid that it was much overrated. Unless the motor would develop a full 8 brake horse power, it would be useless for our purpose.

Finally we decided to undertake the building of the motor ourselves. We estimated that we could make one of four cylinders with 4 inch bore and 4 inch stroke, weighing not over two hundred pounds, including all accessories. Our only experience up to that time in the building of gasoline motors had been in the construction of an air-cooled motor, 5 inch bore and 7 inch stroke, which was used to run the machinery of our small workshop. To be certain that four cylinders of the size we had adopted (4" x 4") would develop the necessary 8 horse power, we first fitted them into a temporary frame of simple and cheap construction. In just six weeks from the time the design was started, we had the motor on the block testing its power. The ability to do this so quickly was largely due to the enthusiastic and efficient services of Mr. C. E. Taylor, who did all the machine work in our shop for the first as well as the succeeding experimental machines. There was no provision for lubricating either cylinders or bearings while this motor was running. For that reason it was not possible to run it more than a minute or two at a time. In these short tests the motor developed about nine horse power. We were then satisfied that, with proper lubrication and better adjustments, a little more power could be expected. The completion of the motor according to drawing was, therefore, proceeded with at once.

While Mr. Taylor was engaged with this work, Wilbur and I were busy in completing the design of the machine itself. The preliminary tests of the motor having convinced us that more than 8 horse power would be secured, we felt free to add enough weight to build a more substantial machine than we had originally contemplated.

Our tables of air pressures and our experience in flying with the 1902 glider, enabled us, we thought, to calculate exactly the thrust necessary to sustain the machine in flight. But to design a propeller that would give this thrust with the power we had at our command, was a matter we had not as yet seriously considered. No data on air propellers was available, but we had always understood that it was not a difficult matter to secure an efficiency of 50% with marine propellers. All that would be necessary would be to learn the theory of the operation of marine propellers from books on marine engineering, and then substitute air pressures for water pressures. Accordingly we secured several such books from the Dayton Public Library. Much to our surprise, all the formulae on propellers contained in these books were of an empirical nature. There was no way of adapting them to calculations of aerial propellers. As we could afford neither the time nor expense of a long series of experiments to find by trial a propeller suitable for our machine, we decided to rely more on theory than was the practice with marine engineers.

It was apparent that a propeller was simply an aeroplane traveling in a spiral course. As we could calculate the effect of an aeroplane traveling in a straight course, why should we not be able to calculate the effect of one traveling in a spiral course? At first glance this does not appear difficult, but on further consideration it is hard to find even a point from which to make a start; for nothing about a propeller, or the medium in which it acts, stands still for a moment. The thrust depends upon the speed and the angle at which the blade strikes the air; the angle at which the blade strikes the air depends upon the speed at which the propeller is turning, the speed the machine is traveling forward, and the speed at which the air is slipping backward; the slip of the air backward depends upon the thrust exerted by the propeller, and the amount of air acted upon. When any one of these changes, it changes all the rest, as they are all interdependent upon one another. But these are only a few of the many factors that must be considered and determined in calculating and designing propellers. Our minds became so obsessed with it that we could do little other work. We engaged in innumerable discussions, and often after an hour or so of heated argument, we would discover that we were as far from agreement as when we started, but that both had changed to the other's original position in the discussion. After a couple of months of this study and discussion, we were able to follow the various reactions in their intricate relations long enough to begin to understand them. We realized that the thrust generated by a propeller when standing stationary was no indication of the thrust when in motion. The only way to really test the efficiency of a propeller would be to actually try it on the machine.

For two reasons we decided to use two propellers. In the first place we could, by the use of two propellers, secure a reaction against a greater quantity of air, and at the same time use a larger pitch angle than was possible with one propeller; and in the second place by having the propellors turn in opposite direction, the gyroscopic action of one would neutralize that of the other. The method we adopted of driving the propellers in opposite directions by means of chains is now too well known to need description here. We decided to place the motor to one side of the man, so that in case of a plunge headfirst, the motor could not fall upon him. In our gliding experiments we had had a number of experiences in which we had landed upon one wing, but the crushing of the wing had absorbed the shock, so that we were not uneasy about the motor in case of a landing of that kind. To provide against the machine rolling over forward in landing, we designed skids like sled runners, extending out in front of the main surfaces. Otherwise the general construction and operation of the machine was to be similar to that of the 1902 glider.

When the motor was completed and tested, we found that it would develop sixteen horse power for a few seconds, but that the power rapidly dropped till, at the end of a minute, it was only 12 horse power. Ignorant of what a motor of this size ought to develop, we were greatly pleased with its performance. More experience showed us that we did not get one-half of the power we should have had.

With twelve horse power at our command, we considered that we could permit the weight of the machine with operator to rise to 750 or 800 pounds, and still have as much surplus power as we had originally allowed for in the first estimate of 550 pounds.

Before leaving for our camp at Kitty Hawk we tested the chain drive for the propellers in our shop at Dayton, and found it satisfactory. We found, however, that our first propeller shafts, which were constructed of heavy gauge steel tubing, were not strong enough to stand the shocks received from a gasoline motor with light fly wheel, although they would have been able to transmit three or four times the power uniformly applied. We therefore built a new set of shafts of heavier tubing, which we tested and thought to be abundantly strong.

We left Dayton, September 23, and arrived at our camp at Kill Devil Hill on Friday, the 25th. We found there provisions and tools, which had been shipped by freight several weeks in advance. The building, erected in 1901 and enlarged in 1902, was found to have been blown by a storm from its foundation posts a few months previously. While we were awaiting the arrival of the shipment of machinery and parts from Dayton, we were busy putting the old building in repair, and erecting a new building to serve as a workshop for assembling and housing the new machine.

Just as the building was being completed, the parts and material for the machines arrived simultaneously with one of the worst storms that had visited Kitty Hawk in years. The storm came on suddenly, blowing 30 to 40 miles an hour. It increased during the night, and the next day was blowing over seventy-five miles an hour. In order to save the tar-paper roof, we decided it would be necessary to get out in this wind and nail down more securely certain parts that were especially exposed. When I ascended the ladder and reached the edge of the roof, the wind caught under my large coat, blew it up around my head and bound my arms till I was perfectly helpless. Wilbur came to my assistance and held down my coat while I tried to drive the nails. But the wind was so strong I could not guide the hammer and succeeded in striking my fingers as often as the nails.

The next three weeks were spent in setting the motor-machine together. On days with more favorable winds we gained additional experience in handling a flyer by gliding with the 1902 machine, which we had found in pretty fair condition in the old building, where we had left it the year before.

Mr. Chanute and Dr. Spratt, who had been guests in our camp in 1901 and 1902, spent some time with us, but neither one was able to remain to see the test of the motor-machine, on account of the delays caused by trouble which developed in the propeller shafts.

While Mr. Chanute was with us, a good deal of time was spent in discussion of the mathematical calculations upon which we had based our machine. He informed us that, in designing machinery, about 20 per cent was usually allowed for the loss in the transmission of power. As we had allowed only 5 per cent, a figure we had arrived at by some crude measurements of the friction of one of the chains when carrying only a very light load, we were much alarmed. More than the whole surplus in power, allowed in our calculations would, according to Mr. Chanute's estimate, be consumed in friction in the driving chains. After Mr. Chanute's departure, we suspended one of the drive chains over a sprocket, hanging bags of sand on either side of the sprocket of a weight approximately equal to the pull that would be exerted on the chains when driving the propellers. By measuring the extra amount of weight needed on one side to lift the weight on the other, we calculated the loss in transmission. This indicated that the loss of power from this source would be only 5 per cent, as we originally estimated. But while we could see no serious error in this method of determining the loss, we were very uneasy until we had a chance to run the propellers with the motor to see whether we could get the estimated number of turns.

The first run of the motor on the machine developed a flaw in one of the propeller shafts which had not been discovered in the test at Dayton. The shafts were sent at once to Dayton for repair, and were not received again until November 20, having been gone two weeks. We immediately put them in the machine and made another test. A new trouble developed. The sprockets which were screwed on the shafts, and locked with nuts of opposite thread, persisted in coming loose. After many futile attempts to get them fast, we had to give it up for that day, and went to bed much discouraged. However, after a night's rest, we got up the next morning in better spirits and resolved to try again.

While in the bicycle business we had become well acquainted with the use of hard tire cement for fastening tires on the rims. We had once used it successfully in repairing a stop watch after several watchsmiths had told us it could not be repaired. If tire cement was good for fastening the hands on a stop watch, why should it not be good for fastening the sprockets on the propeller shaft of a flying machine? We decided to try it. We heated the shafts and sprockets, melted cement into the threads, and screwed them together again. This trouble was over. The sprockets stayed fast.

Just as the machine was ready for test, bad weather set in. It had been disagreeably cold for several weeks, so cold that we could scarcely work on the machine some days. But now we began to have rain and snow and a wind of 25 to 30 miles blew for several days from the north. While we were being delayed by the weather we arranged a mechanism to measure automatically the duration of a flight from the time the machine started to move forward to the time it stopped, the distance traveled through the air in that time, and the number of revolutions made by the motor and propeller. A stop watch took the time; an anemometer measured the air traveled through; and a counter took the number of revolutions made by the propellers. The watch, anemometer and revolution counter were all automatically started and stopped simultaneously. From data thus obtained we expected to prove or disprove the accuracy of our propeller calculations.

On November 28, while giving the motor a run indoors, we thought we again saw something wrong with one of the propeller shafts. On stopping the motor, we discovered that one of the tubular shafts had cracked!

Immediate preparation was made for returning to Dayton to build another set of shafts. We decided to abandon the use of tubes, as they did not afford enough spring to take up the shocks of premature or missed explosions of the motor. Solid tool-steel shafts of smaller diameter than the tubes previously used were decided upon. These would allow a certain amount of spring. The tubular shafts were many times stronger than would have been necessary to transmit the power of our motor if the strains upon them had been uniform. But the large hollow shafts had no spring in them to absorb the unequal strains.

Wilbur remained in camp while I went to get the new shafts. I did not get back to camp again till Friday, the 11th of December. Saturday afternoon the machine was again ready for trial, but the wind was so light, a start could not have been made from level ground with the run of only sixty feet permitted by our monorail track. Nor was there enough time before dark to take the machine to one of the hills, where, by placing the track on a steep incline, sufficient speed could be secured for starting in calm air.

Monday, December 14, was a beautiful day, but there was not enough wind to enable a start to be made from the level ground about camp. We therefore decided to attempt a flight from the side of the big Kill Devil Hill. We had arranged with the members of the Kill Devil Life Saving Station, which was located a little over a mile from our camp, to inform them when we were ready to make the first trial of the machine. We were soon joined by J. T. Daniels, Robert Westcott, Thomas Beachem, W. S. Dough and Uncle Benny O'Neal, of the Station, who helped us get the machine to the hill, a quarter mile away. We laid the track 150 feet up the side of the hill on a 9 degree slope. With the slope of the track, the thrust of the propellers and the machine starting directly into the wind, we did not anticipate any trouble in getting up flying speed on the 60 foot monorail track. But we did not feel certain the operator could keep the machine balanced on the track.

When the machine had been fastened with a wire to the track, so that it could not start until released by the operator, and the motor had been run to make sure that it was in condition, we tossed up a coin to decide who should have the first trail. Wilbur won. I took a position at one of the wings, intending to help balance the machine as it ran down the track. But when the restraining wire was slipped, the machine started off so quickly I could stay with it only a few feet. After a 35 to 40 foot run, it lifted from the rail. But it was allowed to turn up too much. It climbed a few feet, stalled, and then settled to the ground near the foot of the hill, 105 feet below. My stop watch showed that it had been in the air just 3½ seconds. In landing the left wing touched first. The machine swung around, dug the skids into the sand and broke one of them. Several other parts were also broken, but the damage to the machine was not serious. While the test had shown nothing as to whether the power of the motor was sufficient to keep the machine up, since the landing was made many feet below the starting point, the experiment had demonstrated that the method adopted for launching the machine was a safe and practical one. On the whole, we were much pleased.

Two days were consumed in making repairs, and the machine was not ready again till late in the afternoon of the 16th. While we had it out on the track in front of the building, making the final adjustments, a stranger came along. After looking at the machine a few seconds he inquired what it was. When we told him it was a flying machine he asked whether we intended to fly it. We said we did, as soon as we had a suitable wind. He looked at it several minutes longer and then, wishing to be courteous, remarked that it looked as if it would fly, if it had a "suitable wind." We were much amused, for, no doubt, he had in mind the recent 75 mile gale when he repeated our words, "a suitable wind!"

During the night of December 16, 1903, a strong cold wind blew from the north. When we arose on the morning of the 17th, the puddles of water, which had been standing about camp since the recent rains, were covered with ice. The wind had a velocity of 10 to 12 meters per second (22 to 27 miles an hour). We thought it would die down before long, and so remained indoors the early part of the morning. But when ten o'clock arrived, and the wind was as brisk as ever, we decided that we had better get the machine out and attempt a flight. We hung out the signal for the men of the Life Saving Station. We thought that by facing the flyer into a strong wind, there ought to be no trouble in lauching it from the level ground about camp. We realized the difficulties of flying in so high a wind, but estimated that the added dangers in flight would be partly compensated for by the slower speed in landing.

We laid the track on a smooth stretch of ground about one hundred feet north of the new building. The biting cold wind made work difficult, and we had to warm up frequently in our living room, where we had a good fire in an improvised stove made of a large carbide can. By the time all was ready J. T. Daniels, W. S. Dough and A. D. Etheridge, members of the Kill Devil Life Saving Station; W. C. Brinkley, of Manteo, and Johnny Moore, a boy from Nag's Head, had arrived.

We had a "Richard" hand anemometer with which we measured the velocity of the wind. Measurements made just before starting the first flight showed velocities of 11 to 12 meters per second, or 24 to 27 miles per hour. Measurements made just before the last flight gave between 9 and 10 meters per second. One made just after showed a little over 8 meters. The records of the Government Weather Bureau at Kitty Hawk gave the velocity of the wind between the hours of 10:30 and 12 o'clock, the time during which the four flights were made, as averaging 27 miles at the time of the first flight and 24 miles at the time of the last.

With all the knowledge and skill acquired in thousands of flights in the last ten years, I would hardly think today of making my first flight on a strange machine in a twenty-seven-mile wind, even if I knew that the machine had already been flown and was safe. After these years of experience I look with amazement upon our audacity in attempting flights with a new and untried machine under such circumstances. Yet faith in our calculations and the design of this first machine, based upon our tables of air pressures, secured by months of careful laboratory work, and confidence in our system of control developed by three years of actual experience in balancing gliders in the air had convinced us that the machine was capable of lifting and maintaining itself in the air, and that, with a little practice, it could be safely flown.

Wilbur, having used his turn in the unsuccessful attempt on the 14th, the right to the first trial now belonged to me. After running the motor a few minutes to heat it up, I released the wire that held the machine to the track, and the machine started forward into the wind. Wilbur ran at the side of the machine, holding the wing to balance it on the track. Unlike the start on the 14th, made in a calm, the machine, facing a 27-mile wind, started very slowly. Wilbur was able to stay with it till it lifted from the track after a forty-foot run. One of the Life Saving men snapped the camera for us, taking a picture just as the machine had reached the end of the track and had risen to a height of about two feet. The slow forward speed of the machine over the ground is clearly shown in the picture by Wilbur's attitude. He stayed along beside the machine without any effort.

The course of the flight up and down was exceedingly erratic, partly due to the irregularity of the air, and partly to lack of experience in handling this machine. The control of the front rudder was difficult on account of its being balanced too near the center. This gave it a tendency to turn itself when started; so that it turned too far on one side and then too far on the other. As a result the machine would rise suddenly to about ten feet, and then as suddenly dart for the ground. A sudden dart when a little over a hundred feet from the end of the track, or a little over 120 feet from the point at which it rose into the air, ended the flight. As the velocity of the wind was over 35 feet per second and the speed of the machine over the ground against this wind ten feet per second, the speed of the machine relative to the air was over 45 feet per second, and the length of the flight was equivalent to a flight of 540 feet made in calm air. This flight lasted only 12 seconds, but it was nevertheless the first in the history of the world in which a machine carrying a man had raised itself by its own power into the air in full flight, had sailed forward without reduction of speed, and had finally landed at a point as high as that from which it started.

With the assistance of our visitors we carried the machine back to the track and prepared for another flight. The stingwind, however, had chilled us all through, so that before attemping a second flight, we all went to the building again to warm up. Johnny Ward, seeing under the table a box filled with eggs, asked one of the Station men where we got so many of them. The people of the neighborhood eke out a bare existence by catching fish during the short fishing season, and their supplies of other articles of food are limited. He had probably never seen so many eggs at one time in his whole life. The one addressed jokingly asked him whether he hadn't noticed the small hen running about the outside of the building. "That chicken lays eight to ten eggs a day!" Ward, having just seen a piece of machinery lift itself from the ground and fly, a thing at that time considered as impossible as perpetual motion, was ready to believe nearly anything. But after going out and having a good look at the wonderful fowl, he returned with the remark, "It's only a common looking chicken!"

At twenty minutes after eleven Wilbur started on the second flight. The course of this flight was much like that of the first, very much up and down. The speed over the ground was somewhat faster than that of the first flight, due to the lesser wind. The duration of the flight was less than a second longer than the first, but the distance covered was about seventy-five feet greater.

Twenty minutes later the third flight started. This one was steadier than the first one an hour before. I was proceeding along pretty well when a sudden gust from the right lifted the machine up twelve to fifteen feet and turned it up sidewise in an alarming manner. It began a lively sidling off to the left. I warped the wings to try to recover the lateral balance and at the same time pointed the machine down to reach the ground as quickly as possible. The lateral control was more effective than I had imagined and before I reached the ground the right wing was lower than the left and struck first. The time of this flight was fifteen seconds and the distance over the ground a little over 200 feet.

Wilbur started the fourth and last flight at just 12 o'clock. The first few hundred feet were up and down as before, but by the time three hundred feet had been covered, the machine was under much better control. The course for the next four to five hundred feet had but little undulation. However, when out about eight hundred feet the machine began pitching again, and, in one of its darts downward, struck the ground. The distance over the ground was measured and found to be 852 feet; the time of the flight 59 seconds. The frame supporting the front rudder was badly broken, but the main part of the machine was not injured at all. We estimated that the machine could be put in condition for flight again in a day or two.

While we were standing about discussing this last flight, a sudden strong gust of wind struck the machine and began to turn it over. Everybody made a rush for it. Wilbur, who was at one end, seized it in front, Mr. Daniels and I, who were behind, tried to stop it by holding to the rear uprights. All our efforts were vain. The machine rolled over and over. Daniels, who had retained his grip, was carried along with it, and was thrown about head over heels inside of the machine. Fortunately he was not seriously injured, though badly bruised in falling about against the motor, chain guides, etc. The ribs in the surfaces of the machine were broken, the motor injured and the chain guides badly bent, so that all possibility of further flights with it for that year were at an end.

The First Eyewitness Account of a Powered Airplane Flight

Amos I. Root Sees Wilbur Wright Fly

On September 20, 1904, Amos I. Root, an enthusiastic apiarist, journeyed to Huffman Prairie, and watched as Wilbur Wright made the first circular flight by a powered, winged aircraft. This flight clearly demonstrated the Wright brothers' mastery of flight, and deeply impressed Root, who was the publisher of a magazine entitled Gleanings in Bee Culture. *Root published his impressions of the flight in an issue of the magazine published on January 1, 1905, pp. 36-39. As in many writings typical of the period, Root used the account to draw moral lessons; its quaintness, however, does not obscure its importance in aviation historiography.*

Dear friends, I have a wonderful story to tell you—a story that, in some respects, outrivals the Arabian Nights fables—a story, too, with a moral that I think many of the younger ones need, and perhaps some of the older ones too if they will heed it. God in His great mercy has permitted me to be, at least somewhat, instrumental in ushering in and introducing to the great wide world an invention that may outrank electric cars, the automobiles, and all other methods of travel, and one which may fairly take a place beside the telephone and wireless telegraphy. Am I claiming a good deal? Well, I will tell my story, and you shall be the judge. In order to make the story a helpful one I may stop and turn aside a good many times to point a moral.

In our issue for Sept. 1, I told you of two young men, two farmer's boys, who love machinery, down in the central part of Ohio. I am now going to tell you something of two other boys, a *minister's* boys, who love machinery, and who are interested in the modern developments of science and art. Their names are Orville and Wilbur Wright, of Dayton, Ohio. I made mention of them and their work on page 241 of our issue for March 1 last. You may remember it. These two, perhaps by accident, or may be as a matter of taste, began studying the flights of birds and insects. From this they turned their attention to what has been done in the way of enabling men to fly. They not only studied nature, but they procured the best books, and I think I may say all the papers, the world contains on this subject. When I first became acquainted with them, and expressed a wish to read up all there was on the subject, they showed me a library that astonished me; and I soon found they were thoroughly versed, not only in regard to our present knowledle, but every thing that had been done in the past. These boys (they are men now), instead of spending their summer vacation with crowds, and with such crowds as are often questionable, as so many do, went away by themselves to a desert place by the seacoast. You and I have in years past found enjoyment and health in sliding down hill on the snow; but these boys went off to that sandy waste on the Atlantic coast to slide down hill too; but instead of sliding on snow and ice they slid *on air.* With a gliding machine made of sticks and cloth they learned to glide and soar from the top of a hill to the bottom; and by making not only hundreds but *more than a thousand* experiments, they became so proficient in guiding these gliding machines that they could sail like a bird, and control its movements up and down as well as sidewise. Now, this was not altogether for fun or boys' play. * They had a purpose in view. I want to stop right here to draw one of my morals. If I allude to myself somewhat, please do not think I do it because I wish to boast. Some of you have read or heard me tell of the time when my attention was first called to bees. Almost the first thing I did was to go to the bookstores and see what *books* were to be found on the subject. I studied these books day and night, and read them over and over again. Then I procured the books and bee-journals from the old world; and when the language was something I could not manage I hired an interpreter to translate for me until I knew pretty nearly what the book contained. In less than one year I was in touch with the progressive beekeepers of the world; and the *American Bee Journal,* that had been dropped for lack of support, was started up again. I mention this to show you that my success in bee culture, from the very first, was not luck or chance. It was the result of untiring energy and work. Now let me draw a contrast. During the years that are past, quite a number of men have come to me with their patented hives. A good many of these men had never seen a bee-journal. Some of them who had paid out their hard earnings to the Patent Office had almost never seen a book on bee culture, and they were not sure, from actual experience, of the existence of the queen-bee. We have inventors at the present time who are giving their lives and money to the four winds in the same poor foolish way. If you wish to make a success of any thing, or in any line among the many lines that lie before us in this great world of ours, find out what the great and good men have done in this special line before you.

Well, these two men spent several summers in that wild place, secure from intrusion, with their gliding machine. When they became experts they brought in, as they had planned to do, a gasoline-engine to furnish power, and made a little success with their apparatus before winter set. As soon as the weather would permit, their experiments were resumed the past season. You may have seen something in regard to it in the papers; but as their purpose has been from the beginning to the end to avoid publicity, the great outside world has had but very little opportunity of knowing what is going on.

---

* When I suggested that, even though sliding down hill on the air was very nice, it must have been quite a task to carry the machine back to the top of the hill every time, the reply was something like this: 'Oh! no, Mr. Root—no task at all. Just remember that we always sail *against* the wind: and by a little shifting of the position, the wind does the greater part of the work in carrying it back,' It just blows it back (whenever the wind is strong enough) up hill to the starting-point.

The conditions were so different after applying power that it seemed at first, to a great extent, as if they would have to learn the trade of guiding their little ship all over again. At first they went only a few hundred feet; and as the opportunity for practice in guiding and controlling it was only a few seconds at a time, their progress was necessarily very slow. Let me digress again just a little.

I do not know exactly how many years ago it was, perhaps something like thirty, that I saw in the *Scientific American* that they had in France what was called at that time a velocipede. As soon as I saw the description I sent an order for one, and I think I had about the first machine in the semblance of a bicycle that was ever in Ohio — perhaps one of the first brought into the United States. The machine cost over $100; and as it was a heavy affair, the express on it cost quite an item more. When it came to hand, after days and weeks of anxious waiting, neither myself nor anybody else could ride it at all. The whole town jeered at me, and the story of the 'fool and his money' was hurled in my teeth so many times I almost dread to hear it even yet. Men of good fair understanding pointed their fingers at me, and said that anybody of good common sense ought to know that *that* thing would not stand up with a man on it, for that would be an utter impossibility. I worked at it, the crowd in my way, for several hours in the morning. Finally I rented the largest hall in the town, went in with one trusty boy who had faith, for a companion, and *locked the door.* After quite a little practice on the smooth floor of the hall I succeeded in riding from one end to the other; but I could not turn the corners. When, after still more practice, I did turn one corner without falling, how my spirits arose! A little later I went in a wabbly way clear around the room. Then my companion did the same thing, and, oh how we did rejoice and gather faith! A little later on, with a flushed but happy face, I went out into the street and rode around the public square. You can guess the rest of it. Well, these boys wanted just the same kind of privacy to try their flying-machine that I needed for my velocipede; but as it measures about forty feet from the tip of one wing to the tip of the other, instead of a large hall they wanted a large level field in some out-of-the-way place. I found them in a pasture lot of 87 acres, a little over half a mile long and nearly as broad. The few people who occasionally got a glimpse of the experiments, evidently considered it only another Darius Green, but I recognized at once they were really *scientific explorers* who were serving the world in much the same way that Columbus did when he discovered America, and just the same way that Edison, Marconi, and a host of others have done all along through the ages.

In running an automobile or a bicycle you have to manage the steering only to the right and left; but an air-ship has to be steered up and down also. When I first saw the apparatus it persisted in going up and down like the waves of the sea. Sometimes it would dig its nose in the dirt, almost in spite of the engineer. After repeated experiments it was finally cured of its foolish tricks, and was made to go like a steady old horse. This work, mind you, was all new. Nobody living could give them any advice. It was like exploring a new and unknown domain. Shall I tell you how they cured it of bobbing up and down? Simply by loading its nose or front steering-apparatus with cast iron. In my ignorance I thought the engine was not large enough; but when *fifty pounds* of iron was fastened to its 'nose' (as I will persist in calling it), it came down to a tolerably straight line and carried the burden with ease. There was a reason for this that I can not explain here. Other experiments had to be made in turning from right to left; and, to make the matter short, it was my privilege, on the 20th day of September, 1904, to see the first successful trip of an airship, without a balloon to sustain it, that the world has ever made, that is, to turn the corners and come back to the starting-point. During all of these experiments they have kept so near the soft marshy ground that a fall would be no serious accident, either to the machine or its occupant. In fact, so carefully have they managed, that, during these years of experimenting, nothing has happened to do any serious damage to the machine nor to give the boys more than what might be called a severe scratch. I think great praise is due them along this very line. They have been prudent and cautious. I told you there was not another machine equal to such a task as I have mentioned, *on the face of the earth;* and, furthermore, just now as I dictate there is probably not another man besides these two who has learned the trick of controlling it. In making this last trip of rounding the circle, the machine was kept near the ground, except in making the turns. If you will watch a large bird when it swings around in a circle you will see its wings are tipped up at an incline. This machine must follow the same rule; and to clear the tip of the inside wing it was found necessary to rise to a height of perhaps 20 or 25 feet. When the engine is shut off, the apparatus glides to the ground very quietly, and alights on something much like a pair of light sled-runners, sliding over the grassy surface perhaps a rod or more. Whenever it is necessary to slow up the speed before alighting, you turn the nose up hill. It will then climb right up on the air until the momentum is exhausted, when, by skillful management, it can be dropped as lightly as a feather.

Since the above was written they have twice succeeded in making four complete circles without alighting, each circle passing the starting-point. These circles are nearly a mile in circumference each; and the last flight made, Dec. 1, could have been prolonged indefinitely had it not been that the rudder was in such position it cramped the hand of the operator so he was obliged to alight. The longest flight took only five minutes and four seconds by the watch. Over one hundred flights have been made during the past summer. Some of them reached perhaps 50 or 60 feet above ground. On both these long trips *seventy pounds* instead of fifty of cast iron was carried on the 'nose.'

Everybody is ready to say, 'Well, what use is it? what good will it do?' These are questions no man can answer as yet. However, I will give you a suggestion or two. The man who made this last trip said there was no difficulty whatever in going above the trees or anywhere he chose; but perhaps wisdom would dictate he should have still more experience a little nearer the ground. The machine easily made thirty or forty miles an hour, and this in going only a little more than half a mile straight ahead. No doubt it would get up a greater speed if allowed to do so — perhaps, with the wind, a mile a minute after the first mile. The manager could doubtless go outside of the field and bring it back safely, to be put in the little house where it is kept nights. But no matter how much time it takes, I am sure all the world will commend the policy so far pursued — go slowly and carefully, and avoid any risk that might cause the loss of a human life. This great progressive world can not afford to take the risk of losing the life of either of these two men. *

I have suggested before, friends, that the time may be near at hand when we shall not need to fuss with good roads nor railway tracks, bridges, etc., at such an enormous expense. With these machines we can bid adieu to all these things. God's free air, that extends all over the earth, and perhaps miles above us, is our training field. Rubber tires, and the price of rubber, are no longer 'in it.' The thousand and one parts of the automobile that go to make its construction, and to give it strength, can all be dispensed with. You can set your basket of eggs almost anywhere on the upper or lower deck, they will not even rattle unless it be when they come to alight. There are hundreds of queer things coming to light in regard to this new method of travel; and I confess it is not clear to me, even yet, how that little aluminum engine, with four paddles, does the work. I asked the question, 'Boys, would that engine and these two propellers raise the machine from the ground if placed horizontally above it?'

'Certainly not, Mr. Root. They would not lift a quarter of its weight.'

'Then how is it possible that it *sustains* it in the air as it is?'

The answer involves a strange point in the wonderful discovery of air navigation. When some large bird or butterfly is soaring with motionless wings, a very little power from behind will keep it moving. Well, if this motion is kept up, a very little incline of wings will keep it from falling. A little *more* incline, a little more push from behind, and the bird or the butterfly, or the machine created by human hands, will gradually rise in the air. I was surprised at the speed, and I was astonished at the wonderful lifting power of this comparatively small apparatus. When I saw it pick up the fifty pounds of iron so readily I asked if I might ride in place of the iron. I received, by way of assurance, the answer that the machine would no doubt carry me easily. You see then I would have the 'front seat'; and even if it *is* customary (or used to be in *olden* times) to accord the front seat to the ladies, I think the greater part of them would say, 'Oh! sit still, Mr. Root. Do not think of getting up to give *us* your seat.'

At first there was considerable trouble about getting the machine up in the air and the engine well up to speed. They did this by running along a single-rail track perhaps 200 feet long. It was also, in the early experiments,

---

* If these two men should be taken away by accident or otherwise, there is probably no one living who could manage the machine. With these men to teach them 'the trade,' however, there are plenty who could doubtless learn it in a few weeks.

found advisable to run against the wind, because they could then have a greater time to practice in the air and not get so far away from the building where it was stored. Since they can come around to the starting-point, however, they can start with the wind even behind them; and with a strong wind *behind* it is an easy matter to make even *more* than a mile a minute. The operator takes his place lying flat on his face. This position offers less resistance to the wind. The engine is started and got up to speed. The machine is held until ready to start by a sort of trap to be sprung when all is ready; then with a tremendous flapping and snapping of the four-cylinder engine, the huge machine springs aloft. When it first turned that circle, and came near the starting-point, I was right in front of it; and I said then, and I believe still, it was one of the grandest sights, if not the grandest sight, of my life. Imagine a locomotive that has left its track, and is climbing up in the air right toward you — a locomotive without any wheels, we will say, but with white wings instead, we will *further* say — a locomotive made of aluminum. Well, now, imagine this white locomotive, with wings that spread 20 feet each way, coming right toward you with a tremendous flap of its propellers, and you will have something like what I saw. The younger brother bade me move to one side for fear it might come down suddenly; but I tell you friends, the sensation that one feels in such a crisis is something hard to describe. The attendant at one time, when a rope came off that started it, said he was shaking from head to foot as if he had a fit of ague. His shaking was uncalled for, however, for the intrepid manager succeeded in righting up his craft, and she made one of her very best flights. I may add, however, that the apparatus is secured by patents, both in this and in foreign countries; and as nobody else has as yet succeeded in doing any thing like what they have done I hope no millionaire or syndicate will try to rob them of the invention or laurels they have so fairly and honestly earned.

When Columbus discovered America he did not know what the outcome would be, and no one at that time knew; and I doubt if the wildest enthusiast caught a glimpse of what really did come from his discovery. In a like manner these two brothers have probably not even a faint glimpse of what their discovery is going to bring to the children of men. No one living can give a guess of what is coming along this line, much better than any one living could conjecture the final outcome of Columbus' experiment when he pushed off through the trackless waters. Possibly we may be able to fly *over* the north pole, even if we should *not* succeed in tracking the 'stars and stripes' to its uppermost end.

SIGNAL CORPS SPECIFICATION, NO. 486.

ADVERTISEMENT AND SPECIFICATION FOR A HEAVIER-THAN-AIR FLYING MACHINE.

To the Public:

Sealed proposals, in duplicate, will be received at this office until 12 o'clock noon on February 1, 1908, on behalf of the Board of Ordnance and Fortification for furnishing the Signal Corps with a heavier-than-air flying machine. All proposals received will be turned over to the Board of Ordnance and Fortification at its first meeting after February 1 for its official action.

Persons wishing to submit proposals under this specification can obtain the necessary forms and envelopes by application to the Chief Signal Officer, United States Army, War Department, Washington, D. C. The United States reserves the right to reject any and all proposals.

Unless the bidders are also the manufacturers of the flying machine they must state the name and place of the maker.

Preliminary.—This specification covers the construction of a flying machine supported entirely by the dynamic reaction of the atmosphere and having no gas bag.

Acceptance.—The flying machine will be accepted only after a successful trial flight, during which it will comply with all requirements of this specification. No payments on account will be made until after the trial flight and acceptance.

Inspection.—The Government reserves the right to inspect any and all processes of manufacture.

GENERAL REQUIREMENTS.

The general dimensions of the flying machine will be determined by the manufacturer, subject to the following conditions:

1. Bidders must submit with their proposals the following:
   (a) Drawings to scale showing the general dimensions and shape of the flying machine which they propose to build under this specification.
   (b) Statement of the speed for which it is designed.
   (c) Statement of the total surface area of the supporting planes.
   (d) Statement of the total weight.
   (e) Description of the engine which will be used for motive power.
   (f) The material of which the frame, planes, and propellers will be constructed. Plans received will not be shown to other bidders.

2. It is desirable that the flying machine should be designed so that it may be quickly and easily assembled and taken apart and packed for transportation in army wagons. It should be capable of being assembled and put in operating condition in about one hour.

3. The flying machine must be designed to carry two persons having a combined weight of about 350 pounds, also sufficient fuel for a flight of 125 miles.

4. The flying machine should be designed to have a speed of at least forty miles per hour in still air, but bidders must submit quotations in their proposals for cost depending upon the speed attained during the trial flight, according to the following scale:

       40 miles per hour, 100 per cent.
       39 miles per hour, 90 per cent.
       38 miles per hour, 80 per cent.
       37 miles per hour, 70 per cent.
       36 miles per hour, 60 per cent.
       Less than 36 miles per hour rejected.
       41 miles per hour, 110 per cent.
       42 miles per hour, 120 per cent.
       43 miles per hour, 130 per cent.
       44 miles per hour, 140 per cent.

5. The speed accomplished during the trial flight will be determined by taking an average of the time over a measured course of more than five miles, against and with the wind. The time will be taken by a flying start, passing the starting point at full speed at both ends of the course. This test subject to such additional details as the Chief Signal Officer of the Army may prescribe at the time.

6. Before acceptance a trial endurance flight will be required of at least one hour during which time the flying machine must remain continuously in the air without landing. It shall return to the starting point and land without any damage that would prevent it immediately starting upon another flight. During this trial flight of one hour it must be steered in all directions without difficulty and at all times under perfect control and equilibrium.

7. Three trials will be allowed for speed as provided for in paragraphs 4 and 5. Three trials for endurance as provided for in paragraph 6, and both tests must be completed within a period of thirty days from the date of delivery. The expense of the tests to be borne by the manufacturer. The place of delivery to the Government and trial flights will be at Fort Myer, Virginia.

8. It should be so designed as to ascend in any country which may be encountered in field service. The starting device must be simple and transportable. It should also land in a field without requiring a specially prepared spot and without damaging its structure.

9. It should be provided with some device to permit of a safe descent in case of an accident to the propelling machinery.

10. It should be sufficiently simple in its construction and operation to permit an intelligent man to become proficient in its use within a reasonable length of time.

11. Bidders must furnish evidence that the Government of the United States has the lawful right to use all patented devices or appurtenances which may be a part of the flying machine, and that the manufacturers of the flying machine are authorized to convey the same to the Government. This refers to the unrestricted right to use the flying machine sold to the Government, but does not contemplate the exclusive purchase of patent rights for duplicating the flying machine.

12. Bidders will be required to furnish with their proposal a certified check amounting to ten per cent of the price stated for the 40-mile speed. Upon making the award for this flying machine these certified checks will be returned to the bidders, and the successful bidder will be required to furnish a bond, according to Army Regulations, of the amount equal to the price stated for the 40-mile speed.

13. The price quoted in proposals must be understood to include the instruction of two men in the handling and operation of this flying machine. No extra charge for this service will be allowed.

14. Bidders must state the time which will be required for delivery after receipt of order.

JAMES ALLEN,
Brigadier General, Chief Signal Officer of the Army.

SIGNAL OFFICE,
WASHINGTON, D. C., *December 23, 1907.*

The Army Advertises For a "Flying Machine"

On December 23, 1907, Brig. Gen. James Allen, the Chief Signal Officer of the U.S. Army, issued Signal Corps Specification No. 486. This landmark document marked the beginning of U.S. military aviation. In 1905, the Wright brothers had offered their invention to the U.S. War Department, but the service's Board of Ordnance and Fortification refused to consider the offer seriously. In 1907, while in Paris, the Wrights had met with Lt. Frank P. Lahm, an Army officer and a noted balloonist. The brothers began a life-long friendship with him and, when he was transferred from the cavalry to the Signal Corps several weeks after first meeting the Wrights, Lt. Lahm became a strong advocate of the brothers. Shortly before Thanksgiving, 1907, Wilbur Wright met with officials of the Army's Ordnance Department and Signal Corps to discuss the possibility of the Wrights furnishing an airplane to the service. He appeared at a formal hearing of the Ordnance Board on December 5, 1907, and stated that the brothers could furnish a heavier-than-air flying machine for a price of $25,000. The result was the December 23 specification, tailored to fit the Wright proposal. To the surprise of the Signal Corps—and the Wright brothers—forty-one bidders submitted proposals. Only two made the required ten percent "good faith" deposit. In any case, only the Wright brothers delivered an actual aircraft for trial: the famed and ill-fated 1908 Military Flyer. The specification is reprinted in full.

The Wright Flyers of 1903, 1904, and 1905

The first three Wright Flyers were uniquely important aircraft. Each represented the highest engineering standards. The 1903 Flyer was the world's first successful airplane. The 1904 Flyer was largely a transition machine between the earlier Kitty Hawk aircraft and the later 1905 Flyer, a fully practical airplane. The following technical descriptions of these three aircraft were written by Charles H. Gibbs-Smith of the Science Museum, London, while he was Lindbergh Professor of Aerospace History at the National Air and Space Museum of the Smithsonian Institution.

The First Powered Wright Flyer, 1903

Justly elated by the success of their last glider in 1902—which incorporated three-axis control—the brothers, in March 1903, applied for a patent based on it: this was granted in 1906. They had already determined to build a powered aeroplane — they did not, as often said, put an engine into one of their gliders — and this machine was constructed during the summer of 1903. But they had to surmount two formidable obstacles before their first Flyer — the name they gave to all their powered machines — was ready for testing: (a) the lack of an available light, yet powerful enough, engine; (b) the provision of propellers. They thereupon designed and built their own 12 hp motor; and — an outstanding achievement — carried out basic and original research to produce highly efficient propellers: they were the first to realize that an airscrew is basically a rotating wing producing "lift" forward of the aircraft.

The first Wright Flyer was a canard biplane having a skid undercarriage, a wingspan of 40 ft. 4 in., a wing area of 510 sq. ft., and a camber of 1 in 20. It had a biplane elevator out front, and a double rudder behind, whose control cables were linked to the warp-cradle. The 12 hp motor drove two geared-down pusher propellers through a cycle-chain transmission in tubes, one being crossed to produce counter-rotation. The launching technique was as follows: the Flyer's skids were laid on a yoke which could run freely on two small tandem wheels along a 60-foot sectioned wooden rail, placed facing into the wind. The machine was tethered while the engine was run up, and then released; when its speed produced sufficient lift, it rose from the yoke and flew. The Wrights did not use any accelerated take-off device, such as a weight-and-derrick, for their 1903 flights. The empty weight of the Flyer was 605 lbs.

After minor but exasperating set-backs at the Kill Devil Hill — where the tests took place — and after brushing up their piloting on the 1902 glider, the brothers made their first attempt on December 14th, 1903, with Wilbur at the controls (he had won the toss of a coin). Owing to over-correction with the elevator, the Flyer ploughed into the sand immediately after take-off.

On the morning of Thursday, December 17th, 1903, between 10:30 A.M. and noon, the first flights were made. After five local witnesses had arrived, Orville (whose turn it now was) took off at 10:35 into a 27 mph wind and flew for 12 seconds, covering 120 feet of ground, and over 500 feet in air distance. On the fourth and last flight, at noon, Wilbur flew for 59 seconds, covering 852 feet, and over a half a mile in air distance. Their speed was about 30 mph. All four take-offs on December 17th were made from flat ground. These flights were the first in the history of the world in which a piloted machine had taken off under its own power; had made powered, controlled, and sustained flights; and had landed on ground as high as that from which it had taken off. No aeroplanes other than the Wrights' could remain in the air for more than 20 seconds until November 1906; it was not until November 1907 that a full minute's duration was achieved by a European machine.

This historic first Wright Flyer was loaned to the Science Museum, London, from 1928 to 1948. It is now preserved in the National Air and Space Museum of the Smithsonian Institution at Washington, D.C., a reproduction being shown in London.

Improved Power-Flying: The Flyer II of 1904

The Wright Flyer II was completed in May 1904, and through the kindness of a friend, an "aerodrome" was set up at the Huffman Prairie, a 87-acre pasture at Simms Station, about 8 miles east of Dayton. The new Flyer had approximately the same dimensions as the first, but had less camber (1 in 20 to 1 in 25), and a new engine of 15-16 hp; the pilot still lay prone, and the warp and rudder controls were still linked. From May 23rd to December 9th, the Wrights made about 80 short flights which enabled the brothers to obtain practice in controlling and maneuvering a powered machine. Some 100 starts were made in all, and various minor setbacks had to be overcome before

consistent and productive flights were achieved. Their total airborne time was about 45 minutes: the longest flight lasted for 5 min. 4 sec. and covered about 2¾ miles. On September 7th they introduced for the first time their weight-and-derrick assisted take-off device, to make them independent of the weather, in view of the small area of the pasture. The most important event was their first circle, completed by Wilbur on September 20th. Circling later became a necessary commonplace, as they did not want to overfly other property. The first circle was the subject of a detailed eye-witness report made and published by Amos I. Root—the first such report in history of a powered aeroplane flight.

There was one control problem still outstanding, a tendency to stall in tight turns, which the brothers did not solve until 1905.

Early in this 1904 season two press visits took place; and, had not the engine failed on both occasions, the history of aviation — and indeed of civilization itself — would have been greatly changed. The reporters never came back, despite every resident in the neighborhood reporting the numerous flights, and soon taking them for granted.

The airframe of the 1904 Flyer II was broken up and destroyed in 1905.

The World's First Practical Aeroplane: The Flyer III of 1905

Although the four brief flights of 1903 have naturally invested the Wrights' first Flyer with the greatest fame, their Flyer III of 1905 — seldom dealt with in aviation histories — should stand equally with it; for the 1905 machine was the first practical powered aeroplane in history. It was of the same general configuration as the others, but differed noticeably in the placing of the elevator farther forward and the rudder farther back to improve longitudinal control. The span was 40 ft. 6 in.; the wing area was slightly reduced, to 503 sq. ft.; the camber was increased to 1 in 20; new sets of propellers were used; but the brothers retained the excellent 1904 engine, a prone pilot position, and also — for the start of the season — the warp and rudder linkage. Its speed was approximately 35 mph. Like all the Wright aircraft, it was deliberately built inherently unstable and had to be "flown" all the time by the pilot. The rudder outrigger was sprung to allow it to hinge upwards if it dragged on the launching rail, or the ground.

The 1905 season at Huffman Prairie lasted from June 23rd to October 16th, and over 40 flights were made. But now the Wrights were concerned with reliability and endurance: they were airborne this season for just over 3 hours. In September they diagnosed the trouble they were having in tight turns as a tendency of the lowered wings to slow up and stall. They cured this by putting down the nose to gain speed while turning. It was in seeking this cause and cure that the brothers took the important step of unlinking the warp and rudder controls, and providing for their separate, or combined, operation in any desired degree.

With this Flyer now perfected, the Wrights made many excellent flights, including durations of 18 min. 9 sec., 19 min. 55 sec., 17 min. 15 sec., 25 min. 5 sec., 33 min. 17 sec., and — on October 5th — their record of 38 min. 3 sec., during which they covered over 24 miles.

The description of this machine as the world's first practical powered aeroplane is justified by the sturdiness of its structure, which withstood repeated take-offs and landings; its ability to bank, turn, circle and perform Figures of Eight; and its reliability in remaining airborne (with no trouble) for over half an hour. It is now preserved in a specially built hall in Carillon Park at Dayton, Ohio.

The Wright Brothers' Engine of 1903

The knowledge of aerodynamics and flight structures that the Wright brothers possessed was not sufficient to ensure them success in developing the world's first powered aircraft capable of sustained and controlled flight. One critical problem was developing a suitable engine to power the craft. The Wrights tackled this difficulty with the same ingenuity that catagorized their other efforts. The following description of the engine that powered the historic 1903 Wright Flyer was written by Robert B. Meyer, Jr., of the National Air and Space Museum. It was a portion of his larger work entitled "Three Famous Early Aero Engines," which appeared in the Annual Report of the Smithsonian Institution for 1961, *pp. 357-372.*

The third of these engines to power an aircraft was that of the Wright brothers during the winter of 1903. Orville and Wilbur Wright designed the engine themselves and built it with the help of their machinist, Charles E. Taylor. It was apparently based on the single-cylinder natural-gas engine they had designed and built previously to power their 1901 wind tunnel.

They began to build it in December 1902, and the first tests were run on February 12, 1903. On the 13th dripping gasoline caused the bearings to freeze, and this broke the engine body and frame. It was necessary to order a new aluminum casting which was received on April 20, 1903. The rebuilt motor was shop tested in May. In a description of the motor by Wilbur Wright dated February 28, 1903, he had this to say:

> We recently built a four-cylinder gasoline engine with 4″ piston and 4″ stroke, to see how powerful it would be, and what it would weigh. At 670 revolutions per min. it developed 8½ horsepower, brake test. By speeding it up to 1,000 rev. we will easily get 11 horsepower and possibly a little more at still higher speed, though the increase is not in exact proportion to the increase in number of revolutions. The weight including the 30-pound flywheel is 140 lbs.

A description of the rebuilt motor by Orville Wright dated June 28, 1903, follows: "Since putting in heavier springs to actuate the valves on our engine we have increased its power to nearly 16 horsepower, and at the same time reduced the amount of gasoline consumed per hour to about one half of what it was before."

By November 5, 1903, the engine had been tested in the Wrights' first powered airplane, the "Kitty Hawk Flyer." Considerable trouble was experienced with the propeller shafts. Finally, new ones had to be made, and so the engine did not become successfully airborne until December 17, 1903.

A detailed description of the motor follows. It consists of quotations from "The Papers of Wilbur and Orville Wright," edited by Marvin W. McFarland.

This historic motor is described by Orville Wright in a undated typewritten memorandum among the Wright papers in the Library of Congress: The motor used in the first flights at Kitty Hawk, N.C., on December 17, 1903, had (four) horizontal cylinders of 4-inch bore and 4-inch stroke. The ignition was by low-tension magneto with make-and-break spark. The boxes inclosing the intake and exhaust valves had neither water jackets nor radiating fins, so that after a few minutes' run the valves and valve boxes became red hot. There was no float-feed carburetor. The gasoline was fed to the motor by gravity in a constant stream and was vaporized by running over a large heated surface of the water jacket of the cylinders. Due to the preheating of the air by the water jacket and the red-hot valves and boxes, the air was greatly expanded before entering the cylinders. As a result, in a few minutes' time, the power dropped to less than 75 percent of what it was on cranking the motor.

The motor was worn in by driving a flat-bladed fan, of approximately five-foot diameter, mounted on the crankshaft. From measurements made in many tests with a stop watch and revolutions counter the speed at which the motor could turn this fan was known. The highest speed ever measured was 300 turns (1,200 r.p.m.) in the first fifteen seconds after starting the cold motor. The revolutions dropped rapidly and were down to 1,090 r.p.m. after several minutes' run.

The crankcase and water jacket were cast in a single block of aluminum alloy. The crankshaft was made from a block of machine steel 1⅝ inches thick and had five babbitted main bearings. A 15-inch, 26-pound flywheel was attached to the rear end of the shaft. A chain drive on the front end drove the camshaft, which operated the breaker arms and exhaust valves. A boxwood idler, 1¼ inches in diameter, without flanges, created tension on the chain.

The valve heads were made of cast iron. The stems were of steel. The intake valves operated automatically. Neither the cylinders nor the pistons were ground. The connecting rods were seamless steel tubes screwed into brass big ends.

The motor was started with the aid of a dry-battery coil box. After starting, ignition was provided by a low-tension magneto, friction-driven by the flywheel. This magneto — permanent horseshoe magnets with exciting coils — weighed 18 pounds. Insulated ignition electrodes in the cylinder heads were connected by a strap of copper. The speed of the motor was regulated on the ground by retarding the spark. A small lever on the leg of the motor controlled the timing of the spark by altering the position of the camshaft. There was no way to regulate the speed of the motor in flight.

Lubrication was supplied to the cylinders by a small oil pump driven by a worm gear on the camshaft. No pump was used in the cooling system. The vertical sheet-steel radiator was attached to the central forward upright. Gas feed was controlled by a metering valve, not adjustable during flight. A shutoff valve, made from an ordinary gaslight pet cock, was placed conveniently near the operator. The fuel tank had a capacity of 0.4 gallon. The fuel line was copper.

The weight of the 1903 engine is given as 161 pounds dry in Orville Wright's letter to Charles L. Lawrence, November 15, 1928, or 179 pounds with magneto. Complete with magneto, radiator, tank, water, fuel, tubing, and accessories, the powerplant weighed a little over 200 pounds.

Orville Wright gave some additional facts in his letter for Fred H. Colvin, March 13, 1945:

> It was entirely disassembled after the flights at Kitty Hawk in December 1903, due to an accident to the crankcase, and was never reassembled until 1916, when it was put together and exhibited with the 1903 plane at the dedication of the new M.I.T. buildings.

On January 9, 1906, Orville Wright wrote Carl Dienstbach in reply to a request for an exhibit at the first Aero Club show in New York:

> We could not furnish the motor used on our original flyer. The water jacket and the main frame have been very much changed; the metal of the old frame has been used in making new castings. We could send you the crankshaft and flywheel of the original engine, but we do not think it would be worth while.

The crankshaft and flywheel were sent, however, and on February 7, 1906, Orville Wright again wrote Dienstbach:

> We are pleased to present the photographs to the Club and would be glad to leave with the Club some relic from our first flyer. We have no objection to the Club's retaining the crank and flywheel for the present, though we wish the privilege of claiming it if we should decide to set the original machine together again, only a few parts of which are lacking. All of the parts of the engine are still in existence excepting the body.

The crankshaft and flywheel of the 1903 motor were not returned by the Aero Club after the exhibit, and when a search was made for them some years later they could not be found. Therefore when the 1903 aeroplane and motor were assembled for shipment to England in 1928, it was necessary to substitute for the missing parts the crankshaft and flywheel of the 1904 motor. A handwritten memorandum among the Wright papers in the Library of Congress (dated 1945 and initialed O. W.) attests to this substitution: "Crankshaft and flywheel of 1904 motor, with modification to fit 1903 chainguide bearing, now in 1903 motor."

Additional information about this engine was furnished by Charles E. Taylor in an article that appeared in the May 1928 issue of the journal "Slipstream." A partial quotation follows:

> Orv and Will then asked me to help them build the motor for their first power-driven machine. They had a little workshop where they built and

repaired bicycles at 1927 West Third Street. As I recall we first hit upon the idea of an air-cooled motor but we decided after some figuring that it would weight more per horsepower than a water-cooled type so we settled upon the latter. I do not know but that if we could have secured the light alloys available today we would have gone ahead with the air-cooled job.

The first thing we did as an experiment was to construct a sort of skeleton model in order that we might watch the functioning of the various vital parts before venturing with anything more substantial. Orv and Will were pretty thorough that way — they wouldn't take anything for granted but worked everything out to a practical solution without too much haste. I think that had a lot to do with their later success.

When we had the skeleton motor set up we hooked it to our shop power, smeared the cylinders with a paint brush dipped in oil and watched the various parts in action. It looked good so we went ahead immediately with the construction of a four cylinder engine. I cut the crank shaft from a solid block of steel weighing over a hundred pounds. When finished it weighed about 19 pounds. We didn't have spark plugs but used the old "make and break" system of ignition. The gas was led in and made to spread over the chamber above the heated water jackets and this immediately vaporized it. Of course, we had real gasoline in that day — fully 76 proof and you could count on it going into action at the least excuse.

The cylinders of that first motor were made of gray iron as were the pistons. As I recall those cylinders were from $\frac{1}{8}$ inch to $\frac{3}{16}$ inch in thickness. So far as I know that was the first four cylinder engine ever built. The automobile manufacturers were out of the picture then and the Oldsmobile firm was the only one I was familiar with at that time. We tried to get a motor built there but they couldn't make one near the low weight we wanted. The old one-lunger auto engines of that day really weighed more than our entire flying machine with the first motor installed.

When the engine was ready for block test we rigged up a connection with natural gas, put on a resistance fan and made several block runs in this manner. Later we used gasoline fuel and found the motor would run satisfactorily. That first motor developed around 18 h.p. and weighed around 190 pounds. We were all highly pleased at being able to hold down the weight to this figure but a short time afterward we built another motor that produced around 45 h.p. and which weighed about the same as the first one.

When we installed the first motor in the original machine it lay on its side to the right of the pilot and in such a position that the pilot's weight partially off-set that of the motor. The radiator was made from speaking tubes flattened to reduce the capacity.

Yes, I must admit there wasn't much to that first motor — no carburetor, no spark plugs, not much of anything but cylinders, pistons and connecting rods, but it worked.

SPECIFICATIONS

Cylinders .... 4 horizontal in-line.
Cooling .... Water.
Carburetion .... Surface type — no float.
Ignition .... Low-tension magneto with make-and-break spark.
Horsepower .... 12.05 at 1,090 r.p.m.
Bore and stroke ... 4 x 4 in.
Displacement ..... 201.1 cu. in.
Dimensions .... 13⅝ in. high x 23$\frac{1}{32}$ in. wide x 30$\frac{11}{16}$ in. long.
Weight .... Slightly over 200 pounds including cooling water.
Weight/hp. ratio ... Approximately 16.6 lb. per hp.
Country of
  manufacture .... U.S.A.

In June of 1908 Orville Wright wrote to a friend:

About Christmastime we began the construction of the motor, which is of four cylinders, four-inch bore and four-inch stroke. We had estimated that we would require a little over eight horsepower to carry our weight of 625 lbs. of machine and man. At this weight we would be limited to two hundred lbs. for our motor. Our motor on completion turned out to be a very pleasant surprise. instead of eight horsepower, for which we hoped but hardly expected, it has given us 13 (non-continuous) horsepower on the brake, with a (dry) weight of only 150 lbs. in the motor.

In 1904 we built two more motors of the design of 1903, excepting that an extra half inch of water was provided for over the cylinders. One of these motors was of four-inch bore.... The four-inch bore motor was experimented with in the shop in 1904, 1905, and 1906, and finally was developed to the point where it would hold 24 to 25 horsepower continuously at 1,300 revolutions per minuite. This was just twice the power secured from the original motor of the same size....

Although the 1903 Wright brothers' motor was heavier for the horsepower it delivered than those of Santos Dumont or Professor Langley (respectively two and four times as heavy), it nevertheless fulfilled its function. On April 12, 1911, Orville Wright wrote: "We look upon reliability in running as of much more more importance than lightness of weight in aeroplane motors. We attempt to design our flyers of such efficiency that extremely light motors are not needed."

Since the Wright brothers did not have the wealth of Santos Dumont or the Government grant of Langley, it was necessary for them to build their own engine. It therefore had to be of practical and simple design. A logical procedure was to adapt the automobile engine to the requirements of the airplane, which is what they did.

A Chronology of The Wright Brothers, 1867-1948

A casual perusal of the lives of the Wrights indicates the energetic pursuit of flight that catagorized all their activities. They had many other interests as well, most technical but some —such as their newspapers —far removed from the shop or laboratory. The following brief chronology highlights the activities of the Wrights during the period in which they revolutionized the world. Readers desiring a more complete chronology should consult Arthur G. Renstrom's Wilbur & Orville Wright: A Chronology *(Washington, D.C.: Library of Congress, 1975). This excellent work, commemorating the 100th anniversary of the birth of Orville Wright (August 19, 1871), is thoroughly researched, and also contains a valuable flight log of the brothers' flights from 1900 through 1918.*

APRIL 16, 1867:
Wilbur Wright is born on a farm near Millville, Indiana.

SEPTEMBER 1868:
Wright family moves to Hartsville, Indiana.

SPRING 1869:
Wright family moves to Dayton, Ohio.

AUGUST 19, 1871:
Orville Wright is born in the family home at 7 Hawthorn Street, Dayton.

1878:
Bishop Milton Wright returns from a trip with a toy helicopter that he presents to the Wright children. It interests the brothers in the study of flight for the first time.

MARCH 1, 1899:
Orville Wright begins publishing the weekly Dayton *West Side News;* a year later, with Wilbur, he converts it into an evening newspaper, *The Evening Item.*

DECEMBER 1892:
Orville and Wilbur Wright open a bicycle shop at 1005 West Third Street, Dayton, later moving to 1034 West Third Street.

OCTOBER 20, 1894:
   The Wright brothers begin publication of a weekly magazine, *Snap Shots.*

1895:
   Orville Wright invents a calculating machine that can add and multiply.

1896:
   The Wright brothers begin to manufacture bicycles of their own design.

1897-1898:
   The brothers study the problem of flight, reading widely. They are particularly influenced by the gliding trials of Otto Lilienthal (1848-1896).

MAY 30, 1899:
   Wilbur Wright writes to the Smithsonian Institution requesting information on aeronautical subjects. His letter is answered by assistant secretary Richard Rathbun, and, as a result, Wilbur Wright orders a copy of Samuel P. Langley's *Experiments in Aerodynamics.*

JULY 1899:
   Wilbur conceives the concept of wing warping for lateral control.

JULY-AUGUST 1899:
   The Wrights build and flight test a biplane kite with a 5 ft. wingspread.

NOVEMBER 27, 1899:
   The Wrights write to the U.S. Weather Bureau for assistance in picking a suitable location for their flight testing research. Willis L. Moore, chief of the bureau, sends information that convinces the brothers to journey to Kitty Hawk, North Carolina.

MAY 13, 1900:
   Wilbur Wright first writes to Octave Chanute, a noted aeronautical pioneer. Chanute and the Wrights subsequently become close friends.

SEPTEMBER 6, 1900:
   Wilbur Wright leaves Dayton for Kitty Hawk. He is joined there by Orville.

OCTOBER 1900:
   The brothers flight test their 1900 glider, then leave for Dayton on October 23.

JULY 7, 1901:
   Wrights return to Kitty Hawk.

JULY 27, 1901:
   Wrights assemble their 1901 glider and fly it for the first time. They fly through August, before leaving for Dayton on August 20. Octave Chanute visited their camp and witnessed many of their flights.

SEPTEMBER 18, 1901:
   Wilbur Wright addresses the Western Society of Engineers, and reports on the results of the brothers' 1900 and 1901 glider experiments.

OCTOBER 6, 1901:
   Wrights test airfoils on bicycle test rig.

OCTOBER-DECEMBER 1901:
   Wrights conduct further tests of airfoils using a wind tunnel and balance of

their own design, employing the test results in their subsequent aircraft designs.

AUGUST 25, 1902:

Wrights leave for Kitty Hawk with their disassembled 1902 glider. They assemble and fly it from September through October, returning to Dayton on October 31, 1902.

OCTOBER 18, 1902:

Smithsonian Secretary Samuel Langley inquires about the Wrights' experiments.

DECEMBER 1902:

Wrights begin construction of the engine for their 1903 Flyer.

MARCH 23, 1903:

Wrights apply for a patent on their aircraft; this patent is issued on May 22, 1906.

APRIL 2, 1903:

In a lecture before the *Aéro-Club de France*, Octave Chanute discusses the Wrights' gliding experiments.

SEPTEMBER 23, 1903:

Wrights leave for Kitty Hawk with their 1903 Flyer. After arrival they begin assembly of the Flyer and also make between 60 and 100 glides with the 1902 glider.

NOVEMBER 4, 1903:

Construction of the 1903 Flyer almost complete. A series of difficulties with the propeller shafts delays the completion of the machine until mid-December.

DECEMBER 14, 1903:

First unsuccessful attempt at powered flight by Wilbur Wright; machine stalled after lift-off.

DECEMBER 17, 1903:

At 10:35 a.m., Orville Wright completes the world's first powered, sustained, and controlled flight. A further three trials are completed. Following the last flight, a gust of wind wrecks the machine. The Wrights return to Dayton.

APRIL-MAY 1904:

The Wrights construct their 1904 Flyer, the Wright Flyer II.

MAY 26, 1904:

First flight tests of the 1904 Flyer II, at Huffman Prairie, a 87 acre meadow.

SEPTEMBER 20, 1904:

Wilbur Wright makes first circle in the air by an airplane. This flight is witnessed by Amos I. Root, who subsequently publishes an eye-witness account in *Gleanings in Bee Culture*.

MAY 23, 1905:

Wrights begin construction of their 1905 Flyer, the Wright Flyer III.

JUNE 23, 1905:

First flight tests of the 1905 Flyer III, the world's first practical airplane, at Huffman Prairie.

OCTOBER 9, 1905:
> The Wrights write to the Secretary of War renewing their previous offers to furnish the War Department with an airplane for scouting purposes. On October 27, the U.S. Board of Ordnance and Fortification declines to take action on the Wright offer.

NOVEMBER 22, 1906:
> The Wright brothers announce that they will not publicly test their aircraft because such tests might jeopardize negotiations for the sale of their airplane.

MAY 16, 1907:
> Wilbur Wright sails for Europe to begin discussions aimed at selling Wright aircraft abroad. He is joined by Orville, who sails for Europe on July 20. At the same time, a Wright Type A Flyer is shipped to France in anticipation of tests, remaining in storage until the summer of 1908.

December 23, 1907:
> In response to letters and discussions with the Wrights, the U.S. Signal Corps issues a specification for a flying machine. On February 10, 1908, the Wright brothers sign a contract with the Signal Corps for delivery of an airplane.

MAY 21, 1908:
> Wilbur Wright sails to Europe to demonstrate the Wright aircraft in France.

July 20, 1908:
> Orville Wright notifies Glenn Curtiss that the ailerons used on the Curtiss *June Bug* are an infringement of Wright wing-warping patents.

AUGUST 8, 1908:
> Wilbur Wright completes the first flight of a Wright machine in Europe, at Hunaudières, 5 miles south of Le Mans.

SEPTEMBER 3, 1908:
> Orville Wright completes the first flight of the 1908 Wright Military Flyer at Fort Myer, Virginia, marking the start of Signal Corps tests of the Wright Flyer.

SEPTEMBER 17, 1908:
> Lt. Thomas Selfridge killed in the crash of the Wright Military Flyer at Ft. Myer, Virginia. Orville Wright, the pilot, is seriously injured but recovers, and goes to Europe to recuperate.

FEBRUARY 3, 1909:
> Wilbur Wright begins demonstration flights at Pau, France.

APRIL 15, 1909:
> Wilbur Wright begins demonstration flights at Centocelle Field, near Rome, Italy.

MAY 13, 1909:
> The Wrights are given a tumultuous welcome by thousands upon their arrival back in Dayton from their European trip. A special two-day celebration in honor of the Wrights is later held on June 17-18, 1909 at Dayton.

JUNE 29, 1909:
> Orville Wright makes first flight of the 1909 Military Flyer at Ft. Myer, Virginia.

AUGUST 2, 1909:
    The Signal Corps accepts the Wright Flyer for military use, the first airplane purchased and placed in service by any government.

AUGUST 8, 1909:
    Orville Wright sails to Germany for the purpose of making demonstration flights and finding a German syndicate to purchase the rights to Wright patents.

AUGUST 18, 1909:
    Wilbur Wright, on behalf of the two brothers, files suit against the Herring-Curtiss Company and Glenn H. Curtiss, charging patent infringement.

AUGUST 29, 1909:
    Orville Wright flies in the Zeppelin airship L.Z. 6 from Friedrichshafen to Berlin with Count Ferdinand von Zeppelin, and later dines with Kaiser Wilhelm II.

AUGUST 30, 1909:
    Orville Wright makes his first flights in Germany at the parade ground of Templehof, near Berlin.

OCTOBER 4, 1909:
    As part of the Hudson-Fulton Celebration, Wilbur Wright flies over the Hudson River from Governors Island to Grant's Tomb and back, before an audience of more than one million New Yorkers.

OCTOBER 8, 1909:
    Wilbur Wright begins instructing the first Army aviators at College Park, Maryland.

NOVEMBER 22, 1909:
    The Wright Company is formed with a capital stock of $1,000,000; Wilbur Wright is president of the company.

MARCH 1910:
    The Wright Exhibition Company is formed, under the management of Roy Knabenshue. It is dissolved in November 1911.

JUNE 29, 1910:
    First Wright Model B aircraft is completed.

OCTOBER 25, 1910:
    Flying the new Wright Baby Grand racing aircraft, Orville Wright attains speeds of 70-80 mph at the Belmont Park Meet.

JULY 15, 1911:
    Orville Wright completes the first test flights of the Wright Model B-1 hydroplane at Simms Station. The B-1 is the first Wright airplane delivered to the U.S. Navy, and arrives at Annapolis, Maryland, for service on July 19.

OCTOBER 16, 1911:
    Orville makes his first glides in the Wright 1911 glider at Kitty Hawk, North Carolina. On October 24, he sets a world's soaring record of 9 minutes 45 seconds, which lasts for a decade.

MAY 2, 1912:
> Wilbur Wright is taken ill in Boston. He returns to Dayton, where it is diagnosed as typhoid fever.

MAY 30, 1912:
> Wilbur Wright dies at Dayton after an illness of one month. Orville Wright subsequently becomes president of the Wright Company.

MAY 1, 1913:
> Orville Wright begins experiments with the Wright CH float seaplane on the Miami River, Ohio.

OCTOBER 15, 1915:
> The Wright Company is sold to a syndicate. Orville Wright continues as a consulting engineer; he sought the sale because he wished more time for personal research.

MAY 13, 1918:
> Orville Wright makes his last flight as a pilot, flying a 1911 Wright biplane.

JANUARY 29, 1920:
> President Woodrow Wilson appoints Orville Wright as a member of the National Advisory Committee for Aeronautics (NACA), founded in 1915. Orville Wright continued to be a member of the Committee until his death.

JANUARY 18, 1926:
> Orville Wright is named as a trustee of The Daniel Guggenheim Fund for the Promotion of Aeronautics, founded by philanthropist Daniel Guggenheim. The Fund continues in operation from 1926 until 1930.

MARCH 2, 1927:
> President Calvin Coolidge signs legislation providing for the erection of a monument at Kill Devil Hill in honor of the Wrights.

OCTOBER 12, 1927:
> The Army Air Corps dedicates Wright Field, Dayton, Ohio, in honor of Wilbur and Orville Wright. It subsequently becomes a major research and development center.

JANUARY 31, 1928:
> The original 1903 Wright Flyer is shipped to England for exhibition at the Science Museum.

DECEMBER 17, 1928:
> On the 25th anniversary of the epochal Wright flight of 1903, ceremonies are held at Kitty Hawk, including the laying of the cornerstone of the Wright monument.

NOVEMBER 19, 1932:
> A 60-foot granite memorial is unveiled at Kill Devil Hill, Kitty Hawk, by aviatrix Ruth Nichols. The Wright Memorial's inscription reads: "In commemoration of the conquest of the air by the brothers Wilbur and Orville Wright. Conceived by genius. Achieved by dauntless resolution and unconquerable faith."

OCTOBER 24, 1942:
> The Smithsonian Institution publishes *The 1914 Tests of the Langley "Aerodrome."* This document, containing retractions of earlier statements, ends the Smithsonian-Wright controversy.

JANUARY 30, 1948:

Orville Wright dies of a heart attack while in the Miami Valley hospital, Dayton, where he was recouperating from a previous heart attack.

FEBRUARY 18, 1948:

The coexecutors of the Orville Wright estate announce that in accordance with Orville Wright's wishes, the original 1903 Wright Flyer will be placed in the custody of the National Air Museum, Smithsonian Institution.

OCTOBER 18, 1948:

The Wright 1903 Flyer is removed from exhibit at the Science Museum.

NOVEMBER 22, 1948:

The Wright 1903 Flyer arrives in Washington, D.C., after being shipped across the Atlantic.

DECEMBER 17, 1948:

On the 45th anniversary of the first powered, sustained, and controlled flight, the Wright 1903 Flyer is presented to the Smithsonian Institution.

A Guide to Research

The Wright Brothers

DOMINICK A. PISANO

*I wish to avail myself of all that is already known
and then if possible add my mite to help on the future
worker who will attain final success...*

Wilbur Wright, letter to the Smithsonian Institution, May 30, 1899.[1]

Introduction

One has occasion to wonder if Wilbur Wright could have known, when he wrote these prophetic words at the turn of the century, that they would represent a first step toward a technological revolution so earthshaking that it would change the face of history and the mode of living of entire generations.

In many ways, Wilbur's humble statement applies to those who wish to study the accomplishment of the Wrights and, perhaps, add their mite to the body of knowledge which has accumulated over the seventy-five years since the dawn of powered, sustained, and controlled, heavier-than-air flight. Although much has been written about the life and work of the Wright brothers, fewer and fewer major studies of their achievements have appeared in recent years. The reasons for this neglect are, no doubt, complex, but speculations are in order. Could it be that the advent of later, and possibly more astounding developments in aerospace history have overshadowed their work? Or, has the already formidable body of Wright scholarship intimidated potential researchers who would have otherwise found the area fertile ground for new ideas? One cannot be entirely certain, but whatever the reasons, the story of the Wrights needs to be retold from original and additional perspectives.

For these reasons, a litany of previous Wright research is both unnecessary and unproductive. This paper is intended as a brief and selective review of major published works which will, in turn, direct the reader to more comprehensive sources of bibliographic, biographic, documentary, and photographic information concerning the Wright brothers. Highlighting these areas and suggesting additional topics of research, might well stimulate

---

1. Marvin W. McFarland, ed., *The Papers of Wilbur and Orville Wright*, vol. I (New York, 1953), p.4. Complete bibliographic citations for all published sources which appear in this paper will be found in "Bibliography."

interest in what is the most exciting—and sadly, most neglected—chapter in the history of aviation.

Bibliography

As is often the case with relatively youthful disciplines, bibliographic research in aeronautical history has not kept pace with the demands placed upon it by the ever expanding numbers of books, articles and other published materials which appear every year. Students of the Wright brothers, however, are fortunate to have one of the most meticulously prepared bibliographic tools of its kind in Arthur G. Renstron's *Wilbur and Orville Wright: A Bibliography,* published in 1968 by the Library of Congress in commemoration of the hundredth anniversary of Wilbur Wright's birth.[2]

Proceeding from an abbreviated version of the completed work done in 1952 and 1953 in preparation for the publication of Marvin W. McFarland's edition of *The Papers of Wilbur and Orville Wright,* Renstrom revised and expanded the compilation to approximately 2,055 entries. Although Renstrom's *Bibliography* draws heavily on the extensive Wright aeronautical holdings of the Library of Congress, many supplementary sources and collections were consulted prior to publication. Selectively annotated, the work includes references to books and periodical articles as well as pamphlets, patents, government documents, and court records in eight foreign languages.

Arranged in broad subject categories, the *Bibliography's* major emphasis is on the published writings of the brothers, their interviews, speeches and statements and biographical works relating to their life and work. Succeeding portions of the work are devoted to the Wrights' pioneering experiments in aerodynamics, with emphasis on the wind tunnel, aircraft and flights, 1903 aero engine, automatic stabilizer, control devices, patents and patent suits, Wright companies, and the controversy with the Smithsonian Institution over the Langley Aerodrome.

Of lesser significance, but nevertheless interesting, are references to publications dealing with the monuments and memorials dedicated to the Wrights over the years and the medals and honors awarded them both in the United States and many foreign countries. In addition, there are references to motion pictures, film strips, juvenile publications, memorabillia, art, poetry, etc.

---

2. Researchers should note that the Renstrom bibliography covers through 1967. Although the publication is out-of-print, the Library of Congress's Science and Technology Division will make available, without charge, single copies of the work to requesting libraries.

For supplementary bibliographic material, see J. Laurence Pritchard's more concise, but very acceptable, "A Bibliography of the Wright Brothers," in the March, 1948 issue of the *Journal of the Royal Aeronautical Society* (London).

3. It is interesting to note that, in addition to the Kelly book, the only other biographical work acceptable to Orville Wright was an essay by Alexander Klemin entitled, "The Wright Brothers," which appeared in John Lord's *Beacon Lights of History,* edited by George Spencer Hulbert (New York, 1924), vol. 8, pp. 281-324.

Biography

One of the major problems confronting Wright researchers to date is the lack of a definitive biography. Fred C. Kelly's *The Wright Brothers: A Biography Authorized by Orville Wright,*[3] although long considered the primary biographical work on the subject, does not come to grips with the unconscious experience inherent in the act of creating a practical flying machine, nor does it illuminate the drama of emotional conflict which, of necessity, surrounds those who have left their imprint on the collective consciousness of the world. Moreover, other deficiencies in the book, such the absence of source notes and a bibliography, limit its usefulness to scholarly researchers.

Although John E. Walsh's *One Day at Kitty Hawk* also cannot be considered definitive, it is one of the best sources of new biographical material to have appeared in recent years.[4] Primarily a book of opinion mixed with fact, *One Day* is, nevertheless, one of the first studies of the Wrights to openly challenge what previous researchers have come to accept as acknowledged fact. In this respect, it is one of the most important and most controversial books on the Wrights to have been published in the last decade. A revealing and often moving account, Walsh's book boldly asserts that Wilbur Wright was the intellectual shaper of the brothers' thought, and it is critical of the Kelly biography for "deficiencies and erroneous claims made on Orville's behalf."[5]

Walsh also attempts to distinguish the individual characters and personalities of the brothers, which have had a tendency to blend together in the public mind with the passage of time. Factual and controversial, with well-documented source notes and a rather comprehensive bibliography, *One Day* is mandatory reading for anyone who wishes to gain new insights into the Wrights' story.[6]

4. References to other biographical works concerning the Wrights will be found in Renstrom's *Bibliography,* pp. 13-42.

5. Walsh takes Kelly to task for allegedly misrepresenting a number of facts in the authorized biography. See *One Day,* "Notes and Sources," pp. 252-253; 258; 261; 265; 279; 285-286; 288 and 290.

6. An historical sidelight to biographical studies of the Wright brothers is John R. McMahon's *The Wright Brothers, Fathers of Flight* (Boston, 1930), originally published in 1929 as "The Real Fathers of Flight" in a series of articles appearing in *Popular Science Monthly.* John E. Walsh, *One Day,* p. 253, claims that the book version was only published after McMahon reached an agreement with Orville Wright to alter certain portions of the article text. Based on the so-called Findley manuscript, which Orville had rejected in 1915 as being too personal, the *Popular Science* series was a revision of that earlier manuscript. The co-author of the manuscript, Earl Findley, newspaper reporter and editor and publisher of *U.S. Air Services,* an aeronautical monthly, and longtime friend of the Wrights, had, on more than once occasion, championed their cause, particularly in the dispute with the Smithsonian Instituion over the Langley Aerodrome.

Although the Findley manuscript exists, at least according to Walsh (See *One Day,* p. 5), its whereabouts remain a mystery. Findley, according to *The Wartime Journals of Charles A. Lindbergh,* "had been badly hurt by the whole affair—so badly hurt that it was still somewhat painful to discuss the matter, even after the lapse of a quarter century. I think he was hurt even more by Wright's feeling that the manuscript was unsatisfactory than by the loss of six months' work." (*Wartime Journals,* p. 383) Lindbergh felt that "the manuscript should be extremely

Documentation

The single, most important source in this area is Marvin W. McFarland's two-volume edition of *The Papers of Wilbur and Orville Wright,* consisting of selections from the Wright brothers' collection bequeathed to the Library of Congress in 1949 by the Orville Wright estate. Unlike any other book published about them, *Papers* comprises the most comprehensive body of Wright correspondence, documentation and illustrative material and encompasses every vital aspect of their lives and work from 1895 to 1948.[7]

In addition to the historic Wilbur Wright-Octave Chanute correspondence, which covers the period from 1900 to 1910, *Papers* includes excerpts from thirty-three Wright diaries and notebooks, selections from the Bishop Milton Wright diaries and Wright family correspondence and various papers, lectures, articles and other writings of Wilbur and Orville. Of particular interest are the appendices to each volume, which contain technical material such as a glossary of aerodynamic terms and concepts; information concerning wind tunnel experiments, model airfoils, aero engines and propellers and narrative descriptions and diagrams of Wright aircraft, ranging from the 1899 model glider to the 1916 Model "L" reconnaissance aircraft.

Both volumes are profusely illustrated with photographs, both aeronautical and non-aeronautical, as well as diagrams, sketches, charts and tables. And, as mentioned previously, Arthur Renstrom's short-version bibliography appears in volume two.

Although it was intended for the general reader, *Miracle at Kitty Hawk: The Letters of Wilbur and Orville Wright,* edited by Fred C. Kelly, provides a useful contrast to the *Papers.* Consisting of selections from some 500 letters in the Library of Congress's collection of Wright papers, the book is arranged in chronological order and focuses less on technical matters and more on the autobiographical and personal side of the Wrights. Included are correspondence concerning the Wrights' boyhood and their early interest in the development of a practical flying machine, their experiments in gliding and powered flight and their dealings with the War Department in attempting to sell a useful military aircraft to the United States Army. Interspersed throughout the book are editorial comments by Kelly.

Published in 1977, Patrick B. Nolan and John A. Zamonsky's *The Wright Brothers' Collection: A Guide to the Technical, Business and Legal,*

valuable and should not be lost, even though Findley will not consider publishing it," and he suggested to Findley "that he place the manuscript, sealed, in some library with instructions that it not be opened for twenty-five or fifty years, of for whatever time he thought advisable. I don't know how much impression I made on him, but he said he would consider it. The subject is so sensitive to him that I think I shall not try to press it farther. He says the manuscript is now in a box beside his bed in his Washington apartment." *(Wartime Journals,* p. 447).

7. A description of how the Library of Congress came to acquire and publish the Wright papers will be found in Marvin McFarland's comprehensive introduction to the *Papers,* vol. I, pp. vii-xxiii. In addition to an unpublished finding aid in the Library's Manuscript Division, the Wright papers are described in *The Library of Congress Quarterly Journal of Current Acquisitions,* August, 1950, pp. 22-34.

Genealogical, Photographic and Other Archives at Wright State University, provides a detailed description of all of the materials in the Wright estate not acquired by the Library of Congress in 1949.[8]

Noteworthy among the aeronautical papers in the Wright State collection in Dayton, Ohio, are the Langley Aerodrome files which deal with Glenn Curtiss's modification of the machine in 1914; the Wright versus Herring-Curtiss patent suit documentation and correspondence between the Wrights and Hart O. Berg, the representative of Flint and Company, the agent in contract negotiations for the sale of Wright machines in Europe. In addition to these primary aeronautical materials, are the early Wright company catalogs (1910-1913) which provide information concerning the types of aircraft marketed by the Wrights and particulars of the Wright flying school.

Among the non-aeronautical materials and papers are the personal writings and records of the brothers and the Wright family. Included are such items as the Wrights' private publications and humorous ephemera, carefully detailed financial records of business, personal and household accounts dating from the days of the Wright Cycle Company to the death of Orville in 1948, and newspaper clippings relating to the Wrights' activities from 1903 to 1910 and 1927 to 1949.

Supplementing the non--aeronautical materials are the Bishop Milton Wright Papers, consisting not only of church documents, letters and religious pamphlets relating to his ministry, but also manuscript diaries, begun in 1857, in which are recorded data pertinent to the Wrights' aeronautical experiments and flying activities. In addition, the Bishop's (and later, Orville's) genealogical correspondence, notes and other papers document the various branches of the Wright family tree.

Completing the Nolan-Zamonsky book is a description of the Wrights' technical library collection, many of whose books, journals and pamphlets contain personally inscribed marginal notes and lineations. Finally, there are the recognitions and memorabilia, consisting of awards, citations, travel records and sound recordings which pertain to many aspects of the Wrights' career.

Many little-known collections of Wright papers, photographs and other materials, as well as all of the more familiar repositories, will be found in Lawrence Paszek's extremely valuable, *United States Air Force History: A Guide to Documentary Sources.* Although primarily concerned with documentary sources relevant to the study of military aviation, Paszek's book describes Wright holdings not only in Air Force-related collections, but also in many libraries, universities and state historical societies.

In addition to the major collections in the Library of Congress, Paszek also mentions as sources of Wright papers and correspondence, the Frank S. Lahm Papers and Hart O. Berg Scrapbook Collection in the Institute of the

8. A more complete description of how the Wright State University collection differs from the Wright papers in the Library of Congress will be found in the preface to *The Wright Brothers' Collection,* pp. xv-xix.

Aeronautical Sciences Archives, located in the Library's Manuscript Division; the James Means Family Papers at the Harvard University Graduate School of Business Administration in Boston; the General Henry H. "Hap" Arnold and Colonel Ernest L. Jones Manuscript Collections at the Albert F. Simpson Historical Research Center of the Air Force at Maxwell Air Force Base, Alabama; and the Harry A. Bruno Papers in the State Historical Society of Wisconsin in Madison.

Paszek also mentions a number of supplementary collections which may be of interest to Wright researchers. For example, the Aero Club of Illinois Papers in the Chicago Historical Society contain correspondence relating to the Wrights' participation in the 1911 International Aviation Meet in Grant Park. The Franklin Institute Library in Philadelphia maintains drawings of the 1903 to 1905, 1907 and 1910 aircraft, 1910 aero engine and other papers which have to do with the wind tunnel experiments. The Dayton Collection of the Dayton and Montgomery County Public Library has scrapbooks containing newspaper clippings, mementos and brochures, as well as a diary kept by the Wrights' grandmother, Margaret Van Cleve Reeder, with a genealogy, references to the Wright family and other family manuscripts. Also, the D. Bruce Salley Papers in the Louis Round Wilson Library of the University of North Carolina at Chapel Hill, contain a typescript of newspaper stories appearing in May of 1908 which concern the resumption of the Wrights' flying activities at Kitty Hawk after an interval of approximately three years.

Photographs and Motion Pictures

Although sources of published information concerning aeronautical photographs and photographic collections relating to the Wrights are scarce, both Nolan and Paszek review certain of these holdings.[9]

Nolan and Zamonsky's *Wright Brothers' Collection* indexes all of the photographs, both aeronautical and non-aeronautical, in the collection at Wright State University. The aeronautical series consists of original prints made from the Wrights' own negatives at the time when each photograph was taken. In addition to duplicate prints of the original glass-plate negatives bequeathed to the Library of Congress in 1949, the aeronautical collection at Wright State University also contains photographs for which no negatives exist, as well as prints made from negatives damaged in the Dayton flood of 1913. Consequently, many of the photographs in the aeronautical series are unique because they are not duplicated in any existing collection.

Among the non-aeronautical photographs in the Wright State University

---

9. Documentation of a significant Wright photo collection will be available when, as part of the commemoration of the seventy-fifth anniversary of the first powered flight, the Library of Congress publishes *Wilbur and Orville Wright Photographs: A Checklist Commemorating the Seventy-Fifth Anniversary of their First Flight.* The checklist will include photographs which have appeared in various publications, chiefly in serials held by the Library of Congress. Also as part of the commemoration, the Library of Congress will make available on microfiche all of the Wright photographs in its collection.

collection are those of Orville Wright taken with such distinguished persons as Charles Lindbergh, Amelia Earhart and Henry Ford, as well as of the Wright family and Wright memorials and commemorations.

Paszek's *USAF History* lists a number of repositories of Wright photographic and pictorial materials. Of major importance is the Wilbur and Orville Wright Collection in the Prints and Photographs Division of the Library of Congress. Undoubtedly, the most significant group of photographs ever assembled concerning the Wrights, the collection not only contains their original glass-plate negatives, but also an album of corresponding photographic prints, as well as approximately 750 photographs culled from other sources.

In addition to the Wright collection at the Library of Congress, Paszek lists a number of less well-known photographic repositories throughout the country. The United States Air Force Still Photo Depository in Arlington, Virginia, for example, contains various, unspecified photographs of Wright aircraft. Similarly, the collection of the Douglas County Museum in Roseburg, Oregon includes photographs of early experimental aircraft built and tested by the Wrights and the Army at College Park, Maryland, in 1909. The Harold F. McCormick Papers in the Princeton University Library in Princeton, New Jersey, contain photographs of Wilbur Wright. Finally, the Godfrey L. Cabot Papers in the collection of the Massachusetts Historical Society in Boston contain photographs of both the Wright brothers' early aircraft and flights.

Although Paszek only briefly mentions it, the Wright photographic collection in the documentary research files of the National Air and Space Museum, Smithsonian Institution, in Washington, D.C., deserves special consideration. Loosely arranged in a self-indexing filing system, along with other Wright research materials, the museum's collection contains photographs of virtually all of the Wright machines. In addition to Wright aircraft, the collection also includes a number of photographs which depict significant aeronautical events and flying activities, such as the early glider experiments, the Fort Myer trials of 1908 and 1909, and the European flights.

As in the case of photographs, the availability of indexes and other published sources of information relating to aeronautical films of a historical nature is minimal. Nevertheless, Paszek's *USAF History* mentions that copies of films donated by Orville Wright concerning early Wright brothers' flights are available from the Air Force's Central Audio-Visual Depository at Norton Air Force Base, California.

Additionally, the 1977-78 *Directory of Aerospace Education* (published by the American Society for Aerospace Education), one of the few publications to provide information on aerospace motion pictures and film strips available for purchase or rental, lists a five-part Wright brothers' film in black and white. Entitled "History of Flight: The Wright Brothers," the film is narrated by Paul E. Garber, Historian Emeritus of the National Air and Space Museum, Smithsonian Institution, and may be obtained from the Federal Aviation Administration Film Library in Oklahoma City, Oklahoma, and the National Audiovisual Center in Washington, D.C.

Suggested Reading

Space does not permit a review of all of the books, articles and other publications on the Wrights which have appeared since publication of the Renstrom bibliography in 1968. It would be an oversight, however, not to mention some of the more noteworthy among them.

Among the half-dozen titles of major significance, three publications by Charles H. Gibbs-Smith, noted aeronautical historian, stand out. Among these, *The Rebirth of European Aviation*, published in 1974, is unique. It places the Wrights' work in the context of its importance in the revival of what had become a waning interest in aviation in European circles and explores the influence of Wilbur Wright's astonishing mastery of the principles of flight on that reawakening. Of equal importance in discussing the Wrights' place in aviation history from its beginnings to World War II, is his *Aviation: An Historical Survey*, published in 1970. Finally, and still the most indispensable concise study, is his *The Wright Brothers: A Brief Survey of their Work*, originally published in 1963 and amended in 1972.

Arthur Renstrom's *Chronology Commemorating the Hundredth Anniversary of the Birth of Orville Wright*, published by the Library of Congress in 1975, traces, in strict time sequence, the development of significant events relating to the Wrights, from 1867, the year of Wilbur's birth, to 1971, the centennial year of Orville's birth. The chronology includes, among other items, such things as the events leading up to the first powered flight of December 17, 1903, the names of persons associated with the Wrights in both a professional and social capacity, the dates of publication of the brothers' writings on aeronautical experimentation, the dates of applications for aerial patents and of actions taken in the disputes with Glenn Curtiss and the Herring-Curtiss Company and information concerning the bestowal of honors, awards and honorary degrees.

In addition to this wealth of information, the publication also includes a complete log of the Wright brothers' flights with information about the pilot, time, distance, altitude and location, as well as pertinent remarks about the characteristics of each flight, damages sustained by the aircraft, records set or broken, passengers carried and persons in attendance.

Finally, researchers who wish to know more about the Wrights' contribution to early American aviation history should consult Tom D. Crouch's four-part article, "The History of American Aviation, 1822 to 1905," in volume two of *Aviation Quarterly*. And those interested in examining the design features, performance and historical significance of their aero engines should consult Leonard S. Hobbs's *The Wright Brothers' Engines and their Design*, the fifth number in the *Smithsonian Annals of Flight* series.

Directory of Resources

PAPERS, LETTERS AND MANUSCRIPTS

General Henry H. Arnold Manuscript Collection
Lt. Colonel Ernest L. Jones Manuscript Collection
THE ALBERT F. SIMPSON
HISTORICAL RESEARCH CENTER
Air University
Maxwell Air Force Base, Alabama 36112

Aero Club of Illinois Papers
CHICAGO HISTORICAL SOCIETY
North Avenue and Clark Street
Chicago, Illinois 60614

Dayton Collection
THE DAYTON AND MONTGOMERY COUNTY
PUBLIC LIBRARY
215 East Third Street
Dayton, Ohio 45402

Orville and Wilbur Wright Papers
THE FRANKLIN INSTITUTE LIBRARY
20th Street and Benjamin Franklin Parkway
Philadelphia, Pennsylvania 19103

James Means Family Papers
HARVARD UNIVERSITY GRADUATE SCHOOL
OF BUSINESS ADMINISTRATION
Soldiers Field
Boston, Massachusetts 02163

Papers of Wilbur and Orville Wright
Hart O. Berg Scrapbook Collection
LIBRARY OF CONGRESS
Manuscript Division
Thomas Jefferson Building
Washington, D.C. 20540

Harry A. Bruno Papers
STATE HISTORICAL SOCIETY OF WISCONSIN
816 State Street
Madison, Wisconsin 53706

B. Bruce Salley Papers
UNIVERSITY OF NORTH CAROLINA AT CHAPEL HILL
The North Carolina Collection
Louis Round Wilson Library
Chapel Hill, North Carolina 27514

The Wright Brothers Collection
WRIGHT STATE UNIVERSITY
7751 Colonel Glenn Highway
Dayton, Ohio 45431

PHOTOGRAPHS

Photographic Collection
DOUGLAS COUNTY MUSEUM
P.O. Box 1550
Roseburg, Oregon 97470

Wilbur and Orville Wright Collection
LIBRARY OF CONGRESS
Prints and Photographs Division
Thomas Jefferson Building
Washington, D.C. 20540

Godfrey L. Cabot Papers
MASSACHUSETTS HISTORICAL SOCIETY
1154 Boylston Street
Boston, Massachusetts 02215

Wright Brothers Documentary Research Files
NATIONAL AIR AND SPACE MUSEUM
Smithsonian Institution
Washington, D.C. 20560

Harold F. McCormick Papers
PRINCETON UNIVERSITY LIBRARY
Princeton, New Jersey 08540

Still Photography Collection
USAF CENTRAL STILL PHOTOGRAPHIC DEPOSITORY
1361st Photographic Squadron
Headquarters, Aerospace Audio-Visual Service
1221 South Fern Street
Arlington, Virginia 22205

MOTION PICTURES

History of Flight: The Wright Brothers
FILM LIBRARY, FEDERAL AVIATION ADMINISTRATION
P.O. Box 25082
Oklahoma City, Oklahoma 73125

Wright Field Collection
USAF CENTRAL AUDIO-VISUAL DEPOSITORY
Aerospace Audio-Visual Service (MAC)
Norton Air Force Base, California 92405

BIBLIOGRAPHY

Crouch, Tom D. "The History of American Aviation: 1822 to 1905." *Aviation Quarterly*, Vol. 2, No. 1 to Vol. 2, No. 4. Wright material appears in Vol. 2, No. 4, pp. 356-377.

Gibbs-Smith, Charles H. *Aviation: An Historical Survey from Its Origins to the End of World War II.* London, 1970.

Gibbs-Smith, Charles H. *The Rebirth of European Aviation, 1902-1908: A Study of the Wright Brothers' Influence.* London, 1974.

Gibbs-Smith, Charles H. *The Wright Brothers: A Brief Account of Their Work, 1899-1911.* London, 1963, amended 1972.

Hobbs, Leonard S. *The Wright Brothers' Engines and Their Design.* Smithsonian Annals of Flight, No. 5. Washington, D.C., 1971.

Kelly, Fred C. *The Wright Brothers: A Biography Authorized by Orville Wright.* New York, 1943. Paperback edition published by Ballantine Books, New York, 1975.

Kelly, Fred C., ed. *Miracle at Kitty Hawk: The Letters of Wilbur and Orville Wright.* New York, 1951. Reprinted, 1971, New York.

Klemin, Alexander: "The Wright Brothers" in John Lord's *Beacon Lights of History,* vol. 8. ed., George S. Hulbert. New York, 1924, 281-324.

Lindbergh, Charles A. *The Wartime Journals of Charles A. Lindbergh.* New York, 1970.

McFarland, Marvin W., ed. *The Papers of Wilbur and Orville Wright, Including the Chanute-Wright Letters and Other Papers of Octave Chanute.* Vol. I: 1899-1905; Vol. II; 1906-1948. New York, 1953. Reprinted, 1972, New York.

McMahon, John R. "The Real Fathers of Flight," *Popular Science Monthly,* January-June, 1929.

McMahon, John R. *The Wright Brothers, Fathers of Flight.* Boston, 1930.

Nolan, Patrick B. and John A. Zamonsky. *The Wright Brothers Collection: A Guide to the Technical, Business and Legal, Genealogical, Photographic, and Other Archives at Wright State University.* New York, 1977.

Paszek, Lawrence J., comp. *United States Air Force History: A Guide to Documentary Sources.* Washington, D.C., 1973.

Pritchard J. Laurence. "A Bibliography of the Wright Brothers." *Journal of the Royal Aeronautical Society* (London) March, 1948.

Renstrom, Arthur G. *Wilbur and Orville Wright: A Bibliography Commemorating the Hundredth Anniversary of the Birth of Wilbur Wright, April 16, 1867.* Washington, D.C., 1968.

Renstrom, Arthur G. *Wilbur and Orville Wright: A Chronology Commemorating the Hundredth Anniversary of the Birth of Orville Wright, August 19, 1871.* Washington, D.C., 1975.

Walsh, John E. *One Day at Kitty Hawk: The Untold Story of the Wright Brothers and the Airplane.* New York, 1975.

DOMINICK A. PISANO is the Reference Librarian at the National Air and Space Museum. After receiving a bachelor of arts degree from the Pennsylvania State University in 1966, he was commissioned as an officer in the United States Air Force where he held various administrative positions in technical training and aircraft maintenance squadrons. He received his master of science degree in library science from Catholic University in 1974 and is the compiler of "Charles A. Lindbergh: A Selected Bibliography" which appeared in *Charles A. Lindbergh: An American Life,* a collection of commemorative symposium papers published by the museum in 1977.